POKÉMON TRADING CARD GAME PLAYER'S GUIDE

by Brian Brokaw, J. Douglas Arnold and Mark Elies

www.gamebooks.com

SANDWICH ISLANDS PUBLISHING CO., LTD.
POST OFFICE BOX 10669 • LAHAINA, MAUI, HI 96761

PRODUCTION MANAGER . . . . J. DOUGLAS ARNOLD
PRODUCTION ASSISTANTS . . . . MARK ELIES, JAMES YAMADA
EXECUTIVE PRODUCERS . . . . JOE HARABIN, JOAN ARNOLD
OFFICE MANAGEMENT . . . . JAMIE ARNOLD
SALES AND MARKETING . . . . KATHY & JOHN FRUH
COVER ILLUSTRATION . . . . VANESSA ADAMS
ACTIVITIES DIRECTOR . . . . JAMES YAMADA
JAPANESE TRANSLATION . . . . YO TAKEWAKI
POKéMON CONSULTANT . . . . JUSTIN ABILAY
ADDITIONAL ASSISTANCE . . . . DONOVAN PRAIGG, COREY LABORE

We work hard to produce the best books and hope that you love them and tell your friends how cool they are. Be sure to check out our awesome web site at www.gamebooks.com!

99 00 01 - 10 9 8 7 6 5 4 3 2 1

HOW TO ORDER:
For direct orders see the order form in the back of this book or www.gamebooks.com. Quantity discounts are available from the publisher, Sandwich Islands Publishing, P.O. Box 10669, Lahaina, HI 96761; telephone (808) 661-5844 (no gaming tips available at this number!). Fax: (808) 661-9878. Email: sip@maui.net.

Our books are distributed to the book trade by LPC Group.

Printed in the United States of America.

CONTENTS

THE COMPLETE GUIDE

ACKNOWLEDGEMENTS

FROM BRIAN BROKAW

Thanks to Game Freak and Creatures for devising such a fantastic game, and to Wizards of the Coast for bringing it to the U.S. And thanks to all the other aspiring Pokémon Masters out there that have helped turned this addictive card game into a phenomenon! Yes, this means you!

A huge thanks to D for all his effort. I owe him a massive debt for his patience, his encouragement, and his publishing mastery. This book is a tribute to him.

Major kudos to all my buds on the elite_pokélist; Keith Williams, Gordon Kane, Scott Gerhardt, Mark Woodworth, Jonathan Ng, Articuno, Kent D. Kelly, and Steven Diamond. My most sincere appreciation goes out to everyone involved at The PoJo, but especially to a great friend and confidant, Bill Gill. Let me know when the ride stops Butch!

Most importantly, a special thank you to my wonderful Wife and our boys. Nothing would be possible for me without their support, and their love. My work in this guide is especially dedicated to Karla and Brennan—Together they possess all the best that a family can hold, and I constantly strive to follow their path. Thank You!

FROM J. DOUGLAS ARNOLD

Special Thanks to my mom for a lifetime of guidance.

"Whaddups?!" to Lance Ching, Juanito Ancheta, Gavin Campbell, Scott Wery, Willy Campos, Bryan Cruz, Brandon Grant, Grandpa Kidd, Ross Weigand, Al, Kyle Martinez, Ryan, Jeff, Corey LaBore, Donovan Praigg, Nick Bennett, Gregg Abbott, Jeremy Boshart, Gary Gardner, John Ricciardi, Jason Arcangel, Keahi Freeland, Paz Derham, Larry Antonio, Ruth Ko, Adam Dotson, Tom Fernandez, Edwin and Anna at Monster Mega Video Games, Steven "Smike" Henke (and the rest of the Henkes!), Robin Parker, Suzy Brown, Kai McPhee, Nick Wakida, Torian, Ewok, Ilikea, Gizmo, and Willy-pup.

FROM MARK ELIES:

Thanks to my Mother and Father for all their love and support.

Hello to my brothers David, Joel, Daniel, Loren, and my sister Laurie.
Greetings to my sisters-in-laws Shannon and Donna, my nieces Rebecca, Christina, Casey and Morgan, my nephew Conner, my brother-in-law Greg, my Grandparents, my uncle John, my aunt Donna, my cousins Jason, Jon, Shawn, Tonya, Michael and Rachel, my aunt Linda, my uncle Don, Amy, my uncle Danny, James, Floribel, Gordo, Terry, Debbie, Paul, Joey, David, Phil, Jeff, Lucy, and the Soljahs.

EXTRA SPECIAL THANKS

Thanks to Gym Leader Cyndi Jones and the kids at the Kite Fantasy League in Lahaina, Maui for helping us collect all the cards we needed for our Collector's Guides! Especially:

Justin Abilay
Jessica Dempsey
Stephanie Hall
Christine Coshak
Stewart McRoberts
Angel Badua
Luis Hernandez
Augusto "Junior" Castrillon
Joshua Davenhauer
Justin Wolfe

Tori Vorsatz	Lopaka Wilsey	Anson Kaehuaea	Stephanie Hall
Blair Vorsatz	Fernando Moreno	Jessica Wolfe	Casey Sommers
Bruce Kalua	Carlos Moreno	Levi Felt	Kiyo Domogma
Krystlelyn Omlan	Roen Duenas	Stephen Lieu	Blaise Smith
Noelle Potash	Tyler Godfrey	Daniel Phillips	Brent Lopianetzky
Mitchell Pascua	Chris Leverett	Matthew Phillips	Krystle Toribio
James Taasin	Chelsea Drazkowski	Jeff Cabreros	Matthew Spath
Kimberly Suetos	Graham Hennsser	Julian O'Leary	Gus Herrera
Zac Lasco	Micha Spath	Kris Chun	James Villon
Sherwin Pascua	Noah Drazkowski	Shaina Silva	Shai Anna Schamblin
Alexa Lasco	James Huliganga	Riley Silva	Reno Rodrique
Elizabeth Lagbas	Ashley Hayase	Isabelle O'Leary	Devin Weldon
Mychael Lagbas	Jessica Maielua	Cory See	Kaikoa Anderson
Sean Suetos	Tori Dempsey	Samantha Kawaakoa	Naupaka Akau
Glenn Cabreros	Ian Malanog	Marina Desouza	Garrett Nouchi
Dakota Davenhauer	Sione Malamala	Curtis Hinau	Jonathon Perez
Julius Orosco	Kyle Allen	Kamuela Kawaakoa	John Wagner
Sherwin Mitchell	Tyler Stevenson	Allzen Umiat	Alexander Iskenderian
Ivan Saturno	Makena Anderson	Don Gamboa	
Nicholas Falbo	Greyson Kaehuaea	Makani Eisenberg	

INTRODUCTION

WELCOME TO THE WORLD OF POKÉMON! Whether you are a new enthusiast, or someone who has followed the game from inception, Pokémon can be pretty overwhelming! There are literally hundreds of licenses for every conceivable product type for Pokémon fans to pursue. From candy and stickers, to massive movie billboards auctioned off for charity, Pokémon can be a collector's dream as well as their worst nightmare!

What started as a Game Boy game in Japan has taken the world by storm. Billions of dollars have been spent on the Pocket Monsters phenomenon, and its kid's market domination here in North America has just begun to take on speed! From preschool and grade school children up through Parents and Grandparents, Pokémon is quickly becoming a household term. Unfortunately it can sometimes be a term with just as much mystery surrounding it as understanding. This isn't detracting from Pokémon success however, as it continues to show no mercy on homes across the country.

Amidst all the merchandise, the Pokémon Trading Card Game has created a niche for itself with appeal that rivals all the other licensed products combined. True to its Game Boy origins, the Pokémon TCG adds a whole new gaming experience for Pokémon fans to enjoy. Whether it's matching wits with a friend in a Pokémon battle, or collecting that elusive holographic Charizard card, the Pokémon Trading Card Game can be as fun, or even more fun than the original Game Boy cartridges.

As a collector and player, you are bombarded with Pokémon information from thousands of sources. It's sometimes hard to organize it all and make sense of the discrepancies. We understand this frustration and decided to do something about it. Let these books be your ultimate source for accurate and detailed information about the Pokémon Trading Card Game.

Your Guide To Excellence

This strategy guide is exclusively dedicated to the Pokémon Trading Card Game. The Pokémon universe is a vast and cluttered landscape, and without strictly enforcing boundaries our work here would quickly outgrow its binding. Designed as a companion guide to our original Pokémon Trading Card Game Player's Guide, this book covers all the details that were impossible to squeeze into a solitary guide, and expands our in-depth strategy and analysis to blanket the newest U.S. TCG expansion: "Fossil".

Be sure to keep your original Pokémon Trading Card Game Player's Guide handy as you read through this book. Everything included there is top-notch strategy, and a necessary foundation from which the deck lists and single card strategies in this guide build from. There wasn't room to repeat any of the content for our first book here, so a truly comprehensive TCG strategy guide is only complete when they are taken together. Our first book is the only place you'll find:

- Comprehensive game play rules covering everything in the official, advanced level 2-Player game with tons of examples and helpful diagrams. There is even a chapter dedicated to fun rules variations including methods for playing solitaire games!
- The best of the best in strategies and tips to make use of while playing games. Everything from simple advice on keeping track of Pokémon damage to advanced bench manipulation tactics were included.
- A high quality deck construction chapter that takes an incredibly detailed look at the most important factors that drive Pokémon matches to victory. Nothing is "dumbed-down" there and aspiring Pokémon Masters will end up with all the tools they need to build an elite tournament deck.
- Single Card Rulings and Strategies for the U.S. Base set and Jungle expansion cards. From "Abra" to "Zapdos" and "Bill" to "Switch", the

GAMEBOOKS.COM
POKéMON
Trading Card Game
Player's Guide
INCLUDES DECK CONSTRUCTION COLLECTOR'S GUIDE PLUS POKEMON SNAP FOR N64!
BRIAN BROKAW & J. DOUGLAS ARNOLD

first two sets of Pokémon TCG cards are covered in all the great detail that the Fossil cards enjoy in this guide.
- This "Fossil Expansion" version of our Pokémon Trading Card Game Player's Guide series contains all the detailed information that Pokémon collectors and players are pining for:
- A Parent's guide to the Pokémon phenomenon and the Trading Card Game in particular. From one parent to another, this is the stuff that you're so desperate to understand explained in the clearest possible manner.
- A U.S. TCG Collector's guide that details all available information about the existing Wizards of the Coast game cards. From set histories to misprint information, this is an unmatched source for accurate collector information.
- An unprecedented Japanese Collector's guide with full color images of nearly every Japanese regular release cards, and tons of promotional cards as well!
- Detailed single card rulings and strategies for every card released in the U.S. Fossil expansion. Combined with full color images and a useful rating system, this chapter is the ultimate authority for "what's what" in the Fossil expansion.
- A Winning Decks section with 10 completely original and tournament viable decks explored in painstaking detail. Every one of these creations were designed by some of the game's top players to keep you in control and your opponent in the dust!

Our original Pokémon Trading Card Game Player's Guide is still available! Check your local store, use the order form in the back of this book, or call toll free to order: 1-877-490-6770.
Orders Only • No Game Tips or Cards available at this number.

INTRODUCTION

PARENTS GUIDE TO POKéMON

What is a "Pokémon" and where did it come from?

"Pokémon" is the name given to a whole class of unique and make-believe "monsters" that were developed for a video game. These monsters are treated more as loyal and super-intelligent pets than something to be feared. Each monster has a personality and, along with their human "Trainers", will grow in skill and capabilities as the game progresses. All of the popularity surrounding Pokémon originated with the video game and is specifically tied to the fantastic nature of its monsters.

Unlike many less complicated video games, the Pokémon Game Boy games were designed to be almost never-ending. The number of Pokémon first developed for the game numbered over 150 and each one was intricately endowed with descriptive text and statistical abilities. A player continues their game at each session from the exact point in which they previously left off. And because the game was designed for a system that is portable (Nintendo's Game Boy), players can take it with them wherever they go.

The amount of data packed into this Game Boy cartridge is immense! There are literally hundreds of walk-through guides and strategy guides written to describe it, yet nothing even comes close to covering it all! The premise for the video game depicts the main character (you) wandering a strange and mysterious world. As you travel you will randomly encounter wild Pokémon at which point a battle usually ensues between the new monster and a Pokémon belonging to your character. Unlike the more aggressive video games however, Pokémon battles have a rigid code of rules that place tight restrictions on what is acceptable and what is not. No dirty tricks or easy way outs. And unlike those other more violent

games, Pokémon matches never involve the human characters fighting personally, and they never end in any creature's death. The successful end to a Pokémon match occurs when one of the two battling monsters either faints (and is rushed to a nearby Pokémon Center for recovery), or when it is captured by the opposing trainer in a technological marvel known as a Poke Ball.

Pokémon is an adventure game in which your goal is to reach the pinnacle of "Pokémon Mastery". This is the point when all other Pokémon Trainers bow to your skill as second-to-none. This conclusion can only be reached after numerous mini-adventures are resolved and countless hours are spent capturing new and more powerful Pokémon. The game gets progressively harder and certain areas of it are never revealed until the player proves that they are worthy to handle its challenges. As the main character continuously battles with their favorite captured Pokémon, these monsters will grow in power and capability. Each competition will contribute to a Pokémon's development and eventually enable the player to surpass bigger challenges.

With proper training and plenty of experience, many monsters in the game can evolve into different, stronger Pokémon types. The Pokémon Game Boy games were designed to be collectible in nature, and spending time working with your Pokémon to help them evolve is the only way to "catch" many of the 150 you need to be a Master. Another one of the big challenges of the games is to venture out and capture all of the wild Pokémon that are hiding throughout the game. But because the game was intentionally designed to hide certain "rare" monsters, the player will need lots of patience to collect them all. There is an easier way however: two games can be networked together through two Game Boys and a simple cable for

Pokémon TCG Fossil Expansion Player's Guide

trading sessions. If one player happens to be lucky enough to catch an extra rare Pokémon that you might need, negotiate a trade with them so that both of you come away happy!

Pokémon is the English word used to describe the "Pocket Monster" games and products that were originally created in Japan. Everything available here in the states saw its debut up to 3 years previously in Japan. Although the two are synonymous, Pocket Monsters had to undergo some significant translation before making the journey to America. And many industry experts doubted if the Pocket Monster culture could ever be welcomed beyond a very small following in the U.S. Not only has this transition occurred flawlessly, but there has been a continuous shortage of new products on store shelves. Shop owners just can't keep the stuff in stock. Despite any perceived cultural differences, Pokémon helps prove that kids across the globe share more ideas and values in common than not.

Nintendo of America is the master puppeteer for the Pokémon product family here in the United States. Its introduction of Pokémon followed similar lines to the development of products in Japan. First the Game Boy games were released in the Fall of 1998, followed closely by the cartoon series and then the Trading Card Game during that same Winter. And because Pokémon's course has already been plotted in Japan, we are guaranteed at seeing lots of new games, cards, and Poke-stuff in the months and years to come!

Why is it so popular?

Pokémon is a marketing sensation, and that's exactly how it was intended to play out. Kids are being bombarded in all directions, and all at the same time. The multitudes of new video and card games are followed closely by original TV episodes and toys. The cartoon series in particular is intelligently used to educate kids about the games (which tend to be rather complicated in nature), and enamor them with an always increasing product line. And of course, the collectible nature of the entire family of products breeds desire among fans to continuously strive to have more of everything. The Pokémon slogan "Gotta Catch 'em All" was not devised without purpose!

Unlike typical "fads" that gain favor out of the blue and massive popularity overnight, the Pokémon enterprise was well prepared for the demands of instant success. Most existing products available in the U.S. have a long history of sales in Japan to help Nintendo direct the future of the franchise. The video games, TV series, trading cards, and most of the toys have all previously exhibited success overseas. The ability to get all of these elements working together here in the United States has propelled the fervor to unimaginable heights.

Even without all the advertisements encouraging kids to become enthralled with this collectible, many of Pokémon's core features have a strong appeal to younger kids. Unlike other, more standardized collectibles, Pokémon is a game. Its interactive nature allows them a "hands on" approach, in which the nature of their collection is under their control. And, like little sponges soaking up information at a stupendous rate, kids revel in their ability to chat with friends and continually learn more about all the nuances of the Pokémon world.

Far better than some of the more popular fads of the past, Pokémon represents an outstanding theme that kids and adults alike can enjoy. There is no extreme violence. There are no sexual overtones. Simple, cute monsters, with a competitive need to battle make Pokémon the game that parents can feel comfortable sharing with their kids. Girl or boy, parent or kid, everyone seems to find a Pokémon that they can declare as their favorite. This is a welcome hobby for those of us trying to share a passion with our children.

What is a "Trading Card Game"?

Trading Card Games like Pokémon are strategic, engaging, and incredibly addictive. They are based on many of the concepts used in traditional card games like Poker or Rummy. All of the game core game pieces are playing cards and play is turn based between two players. Game play consists of each player taking turns "drawing" a card from their deck into their "hand", choosing which cards to "play" and which cards to keep, and then ending their turn allowing their opponent to complete a turn.

TCGs like Pokémon are not limited to a fixed common pool of cards for players to use during games however. Each player obtains their own collection of game cards, either by purchasing them or by trading with other players.

As a set, there can be hundreds of different cards to select from, each representing different advantages and disadvantages for game play. The TCG player must choose a small subset of these to build their own, personalized play-deck to use. Trading Card Games offer players the opportunity for an immense range of creativity in deck construction, and as a result, an even greater range of variability in head-to-head play. Every game is a fresh challenge with exciting and sometimes unexpected results.

What good is it?

There seems to be quite a few negative stories surrounding Pokémon in the news and media recently. It seems that anything as popular and widespread as Pokémon is surely not immune from becoming associated with some of the bad elements of our society. But does this necessarily mean that Pokémon is bad? Is Pokémon corrupting society, or is society corrupting Pokémon? Here are some personal observations on the game that has turned my household upside down:

I am the "young-at-heart" father of 2 young boys. My oldest son (6 years old at the time) and I began playing the Pokémon Game Boy game together after the Christmas of 1998. He was too young at the time to follow all of the reading required to play this handheld game, so I would read for him and we would take turns playing the game as well. We both really enjoyed it and it gave us a common hobby that we could share and bond with. It was wonderful! (And still is.)

My son's passion for Pokémon has enhanced so-many aspects of his development. The card game has forced him to learn to read, add, subtract, and even multiply. It has increased his sense of fair-play, strategic thinking, competition, and value. And all of these developments have been monitored and actively directed down positive paths by his mother and myself.

Our entire family has been stricken with Pokémon fever. My oldest son and I enjoy the games, while his mother and younger brother enjoy the toys and cartoons primarily. My wife and I can "speak" our kid's lingo and I know that our kids really appreciate that. As a family pursuit, Pokémon has the potential to be incredibly rewarding (and I firmly believe this despite how corny or absurd it may sound).

Most of the problems that have cropped up in the headlines surrounding Pokémon have involved the cards. The cards are marketed as collectibles with inordinate value. The video games, cartoons, toys and comic books are not sold in this way, and do not share the card game's distinction of being perceived a threat to our schools or our children. It is clearly obvious, from reports in the media and from other families, that left unsupervised, the cards do foster some of man's worst qualities: greed, deception, theft, and worse.

However, with supervision, guidance, and involvement, my family has turned the cards into a positive influence on our family. We have a single collection of cards that belong to ALL of us. No one has the right to trade them away without approval of the rest of the family. And, of course, we do not let our kids bring them to school or into any situation where they would cause a distraction.

In the end, the Pokémon cards have the potential to be a very "good" thing. With supervision and understanding, they foster basic reading and math skills in an atmosphere that is exciting for kids. Finding a past time that an entire family can enjoy is difficult enough. Having a past time that excites and encourages kids by challenging the skills they need to grow is wonderful.

What kinds of cards are needed to play the game?

There are many different companies producing licensed (legitimate) Pokémon cards. Topps, Artbox, and Wizards of the Coast are all producing very popular card sets. Even Burger King restaurants have a few sets of Pokémon trading cards to collect. Each of these card sets are different however, and should always be collected separately. This book (and our previous guide) are dedicated only to the Wizards of the Coast cards. These are the only cards that make up the Pokémon Trading Card Game, which is generally the set of cards that enjoy the most popularity. These cards are intended to be a game and encompass a wealth of rules and information that mere trading cards do not possess.

Altogether there are well over 200 different

cards comprising the Pokémon Trading Card Game. Each of these cards are unique, and there is no guaranteed method of obtaining the entire set. After purchasing random "booster" packs and trading furiously with others, every player's collection will be slightly different from another player's collection. Personal preference plays a large factor in which particular cards a player will choose to collect. Just like in the Game Boy game, every Pokémon is unique and despite their desire to catch them all, individual Pokémon players seem to have their own favorites.

The majority of the cards in the Pokémon Trading Card Game set are "Pokémon" cards, and each one depicts a different Pokémon monster (of the original 150 Nintendo Pocket Monster characters released). Many of these are "Basic" Pokémon like Bulbasaur, Charmander, Squirtle, and Pikachu, but others are "Evolved" Pokémon like Venusaur, Charizard, Blastoise, and Raichu. As in the Game Boy game, all Pokémon cards played during a match must begin in their "Basic" stage before evolving into something more powerful. A Pikachu is always required to be in play before its evolution card Raichu can be played, for example. This requirement gives the card game depth and necessitates skill (and a little luck) to yield the appropriate combination of cards during play. Some of the most difficult Pokémon to bring successfully into play are 2nd Stage Pokémon Evolution Cards, like Charizard. However, any disadvantage a player encounters in their efforts to evolve a lowly Charmander up through the 1st Stage Evolution: Charmeleon into the mighty 2nd Stage Evolution: Charizard are well rewarded. Not many defending monsters can survive even a single onslaught of Charizard's "Fire Spin" attack without fainting!

Beyond "Pokémon" cards, there are two other classes of Pokémon Trading Card Game cards, the next being: Energy Cards. There are only 7 different Energy Cards available in the 102 card set, but ironically, Energy Cards are used the most in Pokémon TCG deck building. Any number of duplicates are allowed (and prudent) for basic Energy Cards, and most decks will include approximately 25 to 30 of these. That is a significant chunk of the 60 total cards required in a deck! This large quantity is necessary however, considering that every Pokémon put into play will require a significant amount of Energy cards "attached" to that monster in order to use it's attacks or retreat. Energy allocation is

a major tactical decision that budding Pokémon Trainers must fully understand before they can become true Pokémon Masters.

The 7 different Energy Cards represent each of the 7 different "colors" or "types" of energy used in the card game: Fighting (orange fist symbol), Fire (red fire symbol), Grass (green leaf symbol), Lightning (yellow lightning bolt symbol), Psychic (purple eye symbol), Water (blue tear drop symbol), and Colorless (white star symbol). All Pokémon monster cards are designated as one of these energy types, and typically most of the energy requirements a monster may have for attack moves will match the energy type of the Pokémon itself. For example, Squirtle is a Water type Pokémon and all of its possible attacks require some quantity of Water type Energy attached prior to use. Also, just as in the Game Boy game, Pokémon of certain energy types may have advantages or disadvantages against the opponent's Pokémon type: Charmander's Fire energy type is very strong against Bulbasaur's Grass energy type (Fire burns Grass). But when faced against an opponent's Squirtle (Water type), Charmander better run for cover! Water douses Fire!

The remaining cards in print (beyond Pokémon cards and Energy cards) are classed as "Trainer" cards. Each of these cards can add finesse to a player's deck and really liven up the combat with special abilities documented on the cards. Just like all the Pokémon cards and Energy cards already discussed, Trainer cards are based on different aspects of the original Game Boy game. There are Potion and Full Heal trainer cards to provide mid-combat rejuvenation to a player's Pokémon. There is a Pokémon Center Trainer card to rejuvenate all of a player's Pokémon at once. There is even a "Professor Oak" Trainer card and a "Bill" (the Pokemaniac) Trainer card, both providing the player the ability to dig deeper into their deck, opening up additional options as more cards are revealed. As Trainer cards are drawn during game play, they are typically used once and then discarded. A true Pokémon Master will know which Trainer cards best suit his or her deck and utilize appropriate ratios of these cards, along with Pokémon and Energy cards, to achieve success.

A Pokémon Trading Card Game player will utilize all three different classes of cards (Pokémon, Energy, and Trainer) in building their 60 card play deck. A typical deck will likely contain about 25 "Pokémon" cards with most of those being "Basic" Pokémon, but a few "Evolution" cards thrown in that correspond to some of the "Basic" Pokémon will keep things interesting. Another 25 (or there-abouts) cards should be Energy cards, and finish it off with around 10 Trainer cards. The TCG player is free to change these card ratios to his or her liking, but they must ensure that they have exactly 60 cards in their deck. On top of the 60-card requirement, a further restriction of no more than 4 duplicates of any card other than Basic Energy cards are allowed. This "4 card rule" helps to ensure that games stay somewhat random, and players cannot rely on any one particular card to show up during a match.

Obtaining all of the Pokémon Trading Card Game cards is not required in order to play the game, and some Pokémon TCG cards are easier to collect than others are. Except for basic Energy cards, every Pokémon TCG card will include a rarity symbol on the bottom right corner of the card. Basic Energy are the easiest cards to come by with all starter decks and pre-constructed theme decks shipping with multiple copies of those. "Commons" are the are the next easiest cards to find, leading all the way down to "Ultra-rare" holographic foil cards that are much harder to catch!

Why are some Pokémon cards more popular than others are?

Because this is a card game, each card has value not just for the shiny pictures or the cute monsters, but for their abilities and usefulness in the game. The TCG player will actively seek out multiple copies of the most powerful monster cards for their favorite deck, and chances are that other players will want those same Pokémon included in their deck. Chansey is a perfect example of an all-around great Pokémon that lots of players like to include in their TCG deck. Because its so useful in a variety of situations it has a much higher value to the game player than some of the other holographic cards with the same rarity in the same set (like Magneton! Yuk!)

Of course there are exceptions to every rule and Charizard is a big one! This monstrosity is terrible to play with in the game. Although it looks pretty darn menacing, it is incredibly slow and requires way too much energy to do anything. (These are bad things.) But, any kid who follows these cards will tell you that when it comes to valuable Pokémon TCG cards, nothing tops Charizard. Oh sure, a fire breathing dragon is always bound to bring a yipe of excitement from those lucky enough to pull one from a booster pack, but it hardly seems worth the massive amounts of cash that it consistently pulls in at card shops and online auctions.

How should we start collecting?

The blue box "Starter" deck should definitely be the first purchase made for anyone brand new in the card game and looking to learn the rules. Newer versions of the Starter deck are available with instructional videocassettes or multimedia CD-ROMS. Even collectors who have no intention of playing the game will want one of these Starter decks since they are the exclusive location to find the ultra-rare holographic Machamp card.

Once you have learned the rules and you've decided that playing the game is still your priority, the fastest and most affordable method of becoming a great player is to stick with buying pre-constructed Theme decks at first. Theme decks can be later enhanced with additional cards from booster packs, but starting with a good foundation will be key to a new player's success. Check the U.S. Collector's Guide in this book for a content list for each of the different decks available.

However, collectors who have no interest in playing the game should definitely stick to purchasing only "Booster" Packs. Since the "Pre-Constructed Decks" are specifically designed to play the game, they all include many duplicates of common cards and most of them include only one rare card. This would be a lot of wasted investment to someone only looking to complete his or her collection binder. Also, most of the rare and ultra-rare holographic cards from the different sets can only be found in "booster" packs sold for that set (Basic, Jungle, or Fossil).

How can we identify counterfeits?

The easiest possible method to determine if a card is counterfeit or not, is to compare it very closely to some legitimate cards. Try to buy at least one booster pack from a reputable source that you are sure are the "real deal" (mass market retailers like Toys R Us or Wal Mart are good sources for this). Then compare the suspect card and the legitimate cards very closely. No counterfeits to date can stand up to this kind of scrutiny. They typically have major flaws: they are slightly skinnier than the real deal, or they are missing all the copyright information from the cards, etc.

Another popular test to check for counterfeits is to hold them up to the light, or to bend them slightly. All genuine Pokémon TCG cards are printed on "card stock". This is heavy-duty durable paper that should bounce back into shape when flexed, and should not allow light to pass through it. Again, try to compare the suspect card with a legitimate card so you can easily spot differences when using this test.

However do not misinterpret normal card printing variations with "fakes". These Pokémon TCG cards are produced so fast, and in such high volume that at least 5 different printing factories are involved in making them. This inevitably leads to minor differences in fonts, color shading, stamping, and cutting. Generally, these kind of minor deviations bear no decrease or increase in singles pricing, and do not mean that they are counterfeit.

How can we tell if a trade is fair?

Be sure to check the U.S. Collector's Guide in this book. You will find checklists for the 3 different sets that are available for collecting (Basic, Jungle and Fossil). You will also find a very good description of each element of the cards, along with a very good description of card "rarity". Wizards of the Coast intentionally do not print as many of the rarest cards in order to encourage us all to buy plenty of booster packs! So, rarity is the single most important aspect of Pokémon card trading. Luckily, card rarity is very easy to identify once you know

what you looking for. Trades in which equal rarity cards ("shiny", "star", "diamond", or "circle") are exchanged are usually considered "fair".

However, even though "shiny for a shiny", "star for a star", "diamond for a diamond" and "circle for a circle" is a very good start for fair trading rules, be sure to check into price guides for the cards that you have and need.

Even though Magneton is a "shiny" and Charizard is also a "shiny", you should be able to get about 4 Magnetons for 1 Charizard. This is totally due to popularity of Charizard over Magneton, and you will only figure this out by checking relative singles pricing on the cards. Check www.pojo.com and its monthly publication "PoJo's Unofficial News and Price Guide Monthly", for up-to-date realistic Price Guides.

How can we learn to play?

The Pokémon Trading Card Game is great fun to play, but building your own personalized deck to use can be a little overwhelming at first. Luckily, Wizards of the Coast tried to make playing the game a priority, and have developed a perfect way for new players to get involved. The easiest way to jump right into playing the TCG is to get your hands on one of the pre-constructed "theme" decks. There are currently 9 theme decks to choose from, and each of them come packaged with everything a single player will need: rule book, damage counters, and a 60 card play-deck. All beginning Pokémon Trainers will appreciate the ability to focus on learning how to play a good, strategic game without worrying about collecting enough Pokémon cards to create their own unique deck.

Don't let the fancy packaging fool you; these theme decks pack plenty of power. Each has been designed and finely tuned by the game designers at Wizards of the Coast. They certainly have the ability to make entry-level players competitive in a minimum investment of time and cards. Check the U.S. Collector's Guide in this book for a content list for each of the different decks available.

SINGLE CARD RULES/STRATEGY

Fossil Is Fun To Dig Into!

It doesn't take a Pokémon TCG player long to figure out that the Fossil Expansion is an incredibly fun set of cards to use in battle! Not only does the Fossil expansion finally reveal cards for the remaining monsters from Nintendo's official list of 150. (Monsters that were not previously included in either the original Base set or Jungle expansion.) But a ton of new Pokémon Powers and Attack Move "effects" have been introduced for even more strategic deck construction and game play decisions. Card for Card, there are fewer "dogs" in the Fossil expansion than either of the two previous sets of cards. And this is really appreciated by TCG players everywhere that can be certain that the next set of booster packs they open is bound to house great new cards to capture!

Bench Destruction

Bench Destruction has been evolved with the Fossil expansion into a whole new, realistic theme to rely on. Adding to the few fun cards that previously existed with Self-destruct and selective bench attack moves, the Fossil expansion greatly compounds the threat to any Pokémon TCG player's "safe" benched monsters. And because Weakness and Resistance never apply to benched Pokémon, these attacks can bypass some of the more frustrating match-ups in the game.

There are refinements to some of the previously introduced Bench Destruction techniques—The Self-destruct attack move makes an appearance on a record new quantity of Pokémon, and each of these monsters will have fun with their other attacks right up to the point in which they *explode* and inflict massive quantities of damage for relatively small energy requirements. In addition to some old favorites, there are some fun new bench destruction moves to make use of—Hitmonlee's Stretch Kick and Zapdos' Thunderstorm will reign terror on your opponent's bench without damaging your own. And Articuno's Blizzard bench damage is a hit or miss tactic for an attack move that is already booming with normal attack damage.

Entertaining Pokémon Powers

There is a plethora of new Pokémon Powers to make use of in the Fossil expansion. As is typical for the TCG, most of the more interesting powers reside on rare or highly evolved Pokémon cards. This adds to the excitement of the game without giving too much advantage to a single line of monsters. However, even some of the most basic and common of cards contain powers with outstanding capabilities. Ditto is a rare card, but a Basic Pokémon that can Transform into even the nastiest of your opponent's attackers. In addition, both

Omanyte and Kabuto are common card evolutions to Mysterious Fossil that contain Pokémon Powers that give you a decided advantage over your foe.

There is a grand total of ten new Pokémon Powers in this expansion for Fossil hunters to explore!

Game Boy Concepts

The Fossil expansion will also appeal to Pokémon players that have paid their dues in the original Game Boy games. The card game continues its strong pursuit of remaining true to the source of the craze: the wildly popular Game Boy games. A lot of familiar names will show up in this TCG expansion, and it can be really fun to see how they relate to the original red/blue game cartridges.

In the Game Boy games, the player is confronted with a decision in the depths of Mt. Moon. After defeating a horde of Team Rocket's thugs, the player must choose between one of two Mysterious Fossils as a unique prize. For much of the game afterward, Mysterious Fossil is nothing more than a useless rock in your inventory. However, once you meet the Pokémon Researcher on Cinnabar Island, Mysterious Fossil will evolve into a rare and extinct Pokémon! The Mysterious Fossil trainer card in the Fossil expansion of the TCG plays much the same way: While in play it is a seemingly useless basic Pokémon, with little impact on the outcome of the game—If it is knocked-out, your opponent cannot draw a prize. However, its TCG owner has the option of evolving Mysterious Fossil into one of three unique and interesting Pokémon cards. Just like the hand-held game, Mysterious Fossil's player must make a critical decision on which

evolution to pursue.

Mr. Fuji is a kindly old gentleman that possesses a rare and valuable prize. In the Game Boy games you must first "free" him from the top of the Pokémon Tower in Lavender Town. He gifts you a Pokémon Flute that is necessary to wake slumbering Pokémon that block your path to finishing the game. In the Trading Card Game, the Mr. Fuji trainer card gifts the player with the ability to whisk weakened bench Pokémon back into your draw pile so that their usefulness can live on. This is a valuable gift indeed as it will "steal" a prize from your opponent, and provide the opportunity to bring one of your better monsters back into the game during the rounds that follow.

And just like the previous two sets of Pokémon TCG cards, most of the Pokémon in the Fossil expansion have attack moves that mimic moves you have already seen in the Game Boy games. From Articuno's Blizzard to Weezing's Self-destruct attack move, these monsters really look and feel like those that we grew to love in the red and blue cartridges. But the Trading Card Game also expands the Pokémon universe by adding all new attack moves and Pokémon Powers that have been undiscovered up to this point. For example, while Kabutops's Absorb attack move is identical to that same move available in the Game Boy game, Kabuto's Kabuto Armor Pokémon Power yields a similar result with an all-new set of capabilities. This keeps the Game Boy "feel" to Kabuto, and at the same time expands the card game into all new situations and strategies.

Trainer Card Flexibility

A significant and powerful set of trainer cards accompanies this newest set of TCG cards. Trainer cards are valuable to every deck builder because their usefulness is typically not limited to a particular color of energy or evolution line of monsters. Each of the five new trainer cards has realistic application in many fun and competitive decks. There are no "broken" features presented here to over-power the tournament environment, but all in all balanced cards that help ensure that competitive play stays varied and exciting.

For example, Energy Search is a card that will be much appreciated in multi-color, well-rounded deck compositions. Its ability to speed up these complex decks by enabling just the right color of energy card when it is most needed is balanced very nicely with the detrimental feature of "wasting" a card in order to get that specific energy card out of the draw pile. The multi-color player can now be more confident in their ability to power-up their diversified line up of attackers, and yet the mono-color player can still have the benefit of knowing that they are not using up slots in their 60-card deck on single-use trainer cards.

Winning Single Card Strategies

From Aerodactyl to Zubat, we have the Fossil expansion covered. Full color card scans for every card in the expansion will ensure that you can see for yourself what each card says (and what it doesn't). On top of that, for each and every card, the best of the best in rules, tips, strategies, and winning combinations will make sure that you are prepared to handle all the nuances of this great new set of Pokémon TCG cards. This armory of knowledge was painstakingly collected from tournament champions and industry experts from around the globe.

All single-card and game play rulings have been thoroughly researched from every possible source. You can be certain that the information housed within these pages is entirely accurate and extremely helpful. In addition to game play strategies and useful card combinations, we have rated each card from 1 (a waste of card stock) up to 5 (either you play with these cards in your deck, or you had better prepare your deck to play against them). We have everything you need for your rise to the top of Pokémon TCG Trainers worldwide!

AERODACTYL (LV28)

CARD: 1 (Holo) + 16/62

RATING: 5

RULINGS:

- Prehistoric Power is a "continuous" Pokémon Power, so it never needs to be announced. (It is always "on" unless Aerodactyl is Asleep, Confused, or Paralyzed).
- Prehistoric Power prevents both players from evolving any more Pokémon.
- Pokémon already evolved when Aerodactyl comes into play will not be "devolved" by Prehistoric Power.
- Prehistoric Power will prevent a Grimer from being evolved into Muk.
- A confused Aerodactyl's Resistance will protect it from self-inflicted damage due to failed attacks.

STRATEGY:

- Aerodactyl combines a top-notch Pokémon Power with an all-colorless attack move and Fighting resistance. Many Basic Pokémon intensive decks will find Aerodactyl a great defensive weapon against evolution-heavy opponent's decks. Keep Aerodactyl safe on the bench, forcing your opponent to stagnate while it shuts down all Pokémon evolutions.

COMBOS:

- Aerodactyl + Pidgeot: After you have Pidgeot in play and active, get Aerodactyl on your bench. Now, every time you Hurricane one of your opponent's evolved Pokémon, your Aerodactyl will prevent them from re-evolving it!
- Aerodactyl + Mr. Fuji: Get Aerodactyl in play early in the game to keep your opponent from evolving. Once you have all of your evolution cards in hand and are ready to make your move, use Mr. Fuji on your Aerodactyl to remove it from play. During the same turn you can evolve and start your thrashing!

ARBOK (LV27)

CARD: 31/62

RATING: 3

RULINGS:

- A Pokémon is sent to the discard pile when they have sufficient damage only after all other effects of attacks are complete. So, if Arbok flips a coin: Heads, the active/benched Pokémon swap will occur before the damaged Pokémon is K-O'd. (Damage is placed first, other effects then occur, and finally Pokémon with damage greater than or equal to their Hit Points are knocked out.)

STRATEGY:

- 100% Poison attacks are always a great advantage! The base damage of the attack may be deceiving, but once Poison damage is calculated, the energy requirement doesn't seem quite so steep.
- With only 60 HP and a rather expensive 2 energy retreat cost, be sure to use Arbok to inflict Poison on your opponent before it is K-O'd. After all, Poison is the "gift that keeps on giving" even after Arbok is fainted in your discard pile!

ARTICUNO (LV35)
CARD: 2 (Holo) + 17/62
RATING: 3
STRATEGY:
- In the Game Boy games, the three Legendary Birds (Articuno, Zapdos, and Moltres) are among the most difficult of all the Pokémon to catch! As rare cards, this is only slightly less true in the TCG. As typical for the Legendary Birds, Articuno provides resistance to Fighting, expensive retreats, and powerful (but risky) attack moves.
- Freeze Dry is a decent attack move with the 50% opportunity to keep your opponent's "frozen" and defenseless. Most paralyzing attack moves suffer from low attack damage, but Freeze Dry can finish off even some of the biggest opposing monsters with little resistance (and a few lucky coin flips!)
- Blizzard is Articuno's most efficient attack move. Against an opponent with a bench full of sitting ducks, Articuno has the potential of inflicting 110 damage. And all of that's for only 4 Water energy! It can be difficult to keep this much energy on a single Pokémon however, so be prepared by packing plenty of stalling Pokémon (like Chansey), Energy Retrievals, and a Blastoise or two!

COMBOS:
- Articuno + Blastoise: There is no better way to feed Articuno's insatiable need for Water energy than Blastoise's Rain Dance Pokémon Power. Be sure to keep the Water flowing with a few Professor Oak trainer cards!

CLOYSTER (LV25)
CARD: 32/62
RATING: 1
RULINGS:
- A PlusPower will not inflict 10 damage on Cloyster's opponent if Clamp's coin toss was tails (and Clamp deals no damage). PlusPower only adds 10 damage to attacks that yield additional damage.
- If you flip two tails using Spike Cannon, then this attack will do zero damage.

STRATEGY:
- Low Hit Points, high Retreat Cost, no Resistance all make for a dog of a Pokémon TCG card. And as if that wasn't bad enough, both of Cloyster's attack moves require successful coin flips to yield any benefit! The competitive TCG player knows better than to rely on a coin flip to beat up on their opponents. Reliability should be the key to great tournament winning deck design, and Cloyster just screams "unreliable".
- If using Cloyster to attack, always use Spike Cannon. Clamp averages 15 damage per attack (50% of 30 damage), but Spike Cannon averages 30 damage per attack (50% of 30x2).

DITTO (LV20)
CARD: 3 (Holo) + 18/62
RATING: 3
RULINGS:

- Transform is a "continuous" Pokémon Power, so it never needs to be announced. (It is always "on" unless Ditto is Asleep, Confused, or Paralyzed).
- If Ditto is Gust of Winded from the bench it immediately Transforms (prior to any attacks).
- Ditto will Transform into Clefairy Doll or Mysterious Fossil.
- Ditto will revert to boring old Ditto if a Muk is in play.
- Ditto will revert to boring old Ditto if on your bench, or if it is Asleep, Confused, or Paralyzed.
- When Ditto is Transformed, a Double Colorless Energy card will provide 2 energy of any color.
- Ditto copies everything of the defender's card including Pokémon Powers and discard costs.
- Ditto does not copy damage, ailments, or cards attached to the defending Pokémon however.
- Ditto's owner may not evolve Ditto, but Ditto will Transform to match whatever evolutions that the defending Pokémon undergoes (For example: If Ditto was Transformed to match the defending Psyduck, Ditto's owner may not play a Golduck card on top of Ditto. However, if the defender plays a Golduck card on their Psyduck, Ditto will instantaneously Transform into Golduck.)

DRAGONITE (LV45)
CARD: 4 (Holo) + 19/62
RATING: 2
RULINGS:

- Step In must be declared when used.
- If you flip two tails using Slam, then this attack will do zero damage.

STRATEGY:

- Evolution brings many advantages in Pokémon. In the Game Boy games, Dragonite is said to be highly intelligent and a formidable attacker. Of course you must raise your Dragonair up to level 55 before it will evolve into Dragonite. Perhaps this is why the TCG Dragonite is so weak! It is only level 45! There is virtually no advantage to evolving Dragonair in the TCG. This Dragonite card has an expensive attack that has the potential to inflict no damage, and a Pokémon Power that is hardly a benefit. Since benching a damaged monster does not remove damage counters, Step In will rarely find a good use.

COMBOS:

- Dragonite + Mr. Fuji: If your active Pokémon (not Dragonite) is nearly K-O'd or inflicted with an effect or ailment (like Poison for example), use Dragonite's Step In power to move the damaged monster back to the bench where you can Mr. Fuji all those cards back into your deck and keep your opponent from gaining a prize!

EKANS (LV10)
CARD: 46/62
RATING: 2
STRATEGY:

- Ekans is a pretty mediocre Basic Pokémon with only 40 hit points and no major first turn attacks. Spit Poison can produce lasting results with a successful coin flip, but Weedle's Poison Sting can do the same and provides 10 base damage to boot. Ekans is better utilized with its Wrap attack move—It allows for easy energy

- Ekans does avoid the nasty Weakness to Fire that many Grass decks are so vulnerable to. Now that Fossil Magmar will be popping into so many more decks, any Pokémon that is not weak to Fire is a sound strategy to employ!

GASTLY (LV17)
CARD: 33/62
RATING: 5
RULINGS:

- Double Colorless Energy is an Energy card and can therefore be one of the retrieved Energy cards with Gastly's Energy Conversion attack move.
- Energy Conversion allows the retrieval of 2 Double Colorless Energy cards, or any combination of DCE and Basic Energy cards totaling 2.
- You are allowed only 4 total Gastly in your deck regardless of which expansion they come from. (You are not allowed to include 4 Basic Set Gastly and 4 Fossil Gastly in the same deck).

STRATEGY:

- Wow! What a complete turn around from the Basic set Gastly! Fossil Gastly is a great Basic Pokémon. Its 50 HP ensure that it can survive at least 3 rounds from other early game attackers (who normally Max out at 20 damage per turn). And with no Retreat Cost, Gastly makes an ideal opening attacker (placed during game setup) allowing a quick switch in case the match-up is not to Gastly's liking. Of course with no Weakness, very few match-ups will go against Gastly.

COMBOS:

- Gastly + Item Finder: Item Finder requires the discard of 2 cards from your hand in order to retrieve a valuable Trainer card from your discard pile (like Professor Oak or Super Energy Removal!) With a powered up Gastly active, just discard 2 energy cards from your hand to use your Item Finder. Don't worry! A single Energy Conversion attack and you'll have those energy safe and sound back in your hand.

GENGAR (LV38)
CARD: 5 (Holo) + 20/62
RATING: 5
RULINGS:

- Curse is not an attack, and so Weakness, Resistance, Defender trainer cards, and other Pokémon Powers (like Mr. Mime's Invisible Wall) do not apply to the damage moved using Curse.
- If a Pokémon is knocked-out with Curse, Gengar's Trainer does get to draw a prize card and may still attack during that turn. (Using a Pokémon Power does not stop a Pokémon from attacking.)

STRATEGY:

- Gengar is absolutely evil! (And I mean this in a good way!) Gengar lacks the typical Weakness to Psychic that many Psychic Pokémon possess, but offers Resistance to Fighting! Both Dark Mind and Curse have the ability to attack the opponent's bench making sure that replacement Pokémon don't come out at full capacity.
- Very few Pokémon have the capability of garnering two prize cards in a single round of combat! (And with the right situation, Gengar can sometimes yield three prizes in a single round—One from a Curse onto a Pokémon with only 10 HP left, one from Dark Mind's 30 damage onto the defending Active Pokémon, and one from Dark Mind's 10 damage to a Benched Pokémon!)

COMBOS:

- Gengar + any Poisoning Pokémon: Make the most of Poison inflicted on your opponent and prolong their agony by using Gengar's Curse power to move 10 damage every round onto an un-poisoned Pokémon.

GEODUDE (LV16)
CARD: 47/62
RATING: 1
RULINGS:

- If your first flip is a tails using Stone Barrage, then this attack will do zero damage and your attack is over.

STRATEGY:

- A reasonable quantity of Hit Points and a name that includes the word "dude" are the only real advantages working for this card in the TCG. Stone Barrage is a waste of not just one, but two energy cards! More often than not Stone Barrage will barely nick the opponent, leaving Geodude a sitting duck for more reliable attackers. And if those more reliable opponents are green, Geodude had better run for cover! Geodude's weakness to Grass makes him a prime target for any number of the decent attackers from this class that came to us from the Jungle expansion.
- If Geodude's evolutions (Graveler and Golem) were more appealing, there would be more hope of Geodude seeing play in competitive decks. But as it stands now, Geodude will merely line the binders of even the staunchest of Fighting deck lovers.

COMBOS:

- Geodude + 2-headed-coin: Can you say "infinite damage"? Make sure you switch out the rigged coin when your opponent starts looking suspicious!

GOLBAT (LV29)
CARD: 34/62
RATING: 4
RULINGS:

- Leech Life only counts damage that was actually applied to the defender. So damage that was cut out due to Resistance or a Defender trainer card must not be included in Leech Life's healing ability.
- Leech Life will remove damage from Golbat equal to all damage inflicted, even if less than this total damage was required to knock out the defending Pokémon. (The defender may only need 10 more damage to be K-O'd, but Leech Life still inflicts 20 damage and Golbat gets to subtract all of that from itself.)

STRATEGY:

- Holy multi-functional-Pokémon-cards Batman, Golbat is one heck of a fun Pokémon to play! Leech Life should be considered a very strong attack despite its low offensive damage dealing. Each attack potentially swings the damage race by 40 in favor of Golbat (20 onto the opponent and 20 away from Golbat). And every healed damage point means that Golbat is "turning back the clock" and keeping itself in play longer.
- Be sure to use Wing Attack in situations where Golbat does not currently have damage, or in situation where the extra 10 offensive damage will knock-out the defender and yield another Prize card.

GOLDUCK (LV27)
CARD: 35/62
RATING: 3
RULINGS:

- Even though Psyshock's energy requirement is Psychic energy, all of Golduck's attacks are of type Water (matching Golduck's card). So, Pokémon with Weakness or Resistance to Psychic will not receive extra/less damage from a Psyshock attack.

STRATEGY:

- Ideal in a 2-color Water + Psychic deck, Golduck's Psyshock attack should only be utilized when energy cards are hard to come by. There would be very little advantage to adding Psychic energy in a Water deck just to be able to use Psyshock on occasion.
- Hyper Beam (although extremely energy intensive) is very strong. If your deck can support the time required to develop Golduck (by using more energy efficient attackers or stalling "walls"), Hyper Beam can help eliminate your opponent's ability to counter attack by diminishing their available energy.

GOLEM (LV36)
CARD: 36/62
RATING: 2
RULINGS:
- Every time a Pokémon is K-O'd, that Pokémon's opponent gets to take a prize card. Each Pokémon K-O'd with Self-destruct damage (either Active or from the Bench) will yield a prize to the opposing player.
- A Defender trainer card will protect Golem from 20 self-inflicted damage of Self-destruct, and 2 Defender cards will protect Golem from 40 self-inflicted damage. These Defender cards will still be attached during Golem's opponent's next turn.

STRATEGY:
- Going out with a bang! A Retreat Cost of four energy is a sure sign of a monster that doesn't appreciate being nursed back to health on the bench. And who would bother wasting all of that energy to retreat Golem when Self-destruct is so much more fun!
- Seriously however, Golem is not a highly competitive card. The bench damage infects your own Pokémon as much as your opponent's and Golem's 80 HP is not buff enough to keep it in play long enough to make best use of Avalanche prior to a Self-destruct finale.

GRAVELER (LV29)
CARD: 37/62
RATING: 1
RULINGS:
- Harden does not subtract 30 damage (as Resistance normally does). If an opponent's attack produces more than 30 damage, the full amount is applied to Graveler. Only if 30 damage or less is applied to Graveler will Harden completely eliminate it.
- If Graveler is Poisoned, using Harden will not protect it from the 10 damage per turn Poison that is applied (since this is not damage from an attack—it is damage from the Poison condition).

STRATEGY:
- As a Stage 1 Pokémon, you have to invest a significant amount of time and trouble into evolving your Geodude into a Graveler. Unfortunately Graveler does not repay the favor. Harden is better served on a Basic Pokémon like Onix where it can be used earlier in the game when your opponent's attackers are still dealing 30 damage or less per turn.
- Hopefully a Golem will arrive in your hand shortly after Graveler comes into play. There are better stalling walls in the game (than a Hardened Graveler), and Golem's attacks are much more cost effective than Graveler's Rock Throw.

GRIMER (LV17)
CARD: 48/62
RATING: 4
RULINGS:

- Minimize's effect (reducing damage done to Grimer during your opponent's next turn) will remain for one turn with Grimer even if the Defender is benched. This effect resides with Grimer, and will only go away if Grimer is Benched or Evolved.
- Minimize only reduces damage inflicted from attacks. Poison damage applied at the end of each player's turn is not attack damage, and will not be reduced with Minimize.

STRATEGY:

- Although not a Pokémon TCG card with a whole lot of offensive capability, Grimer is perfectly suited for its primary mission: evolve into Muk.
- Nasty Goo has a colorless energy requirement allowing its use in any color deck. Assuming that Muk will be desired by lots of competitive players to shut down the Rain Dance/Damage Swap combo decks, it's nice to know that Grimer can serve a purpose until Muk arrives in hand.
- In case you don't think that a 50% paralyzing attack (Nasty Goo) is defensive enough, Minimize allows Grimer to stall even more effectively if he happens to find himself as your Active Pokémon. Be sure to carefully consider which of Grimer's two attack moves will provide the desired effect however—inflict a small amount of damage and hope to paralyze the opponent with Nasty Goo, or definitely shut out 20 damage from any opposing attack with Minimize.

HAUNTER (LV17)
CARD: 6 (Holo) + 21/62
RATING: 5
RULINGS:

- Transparency is a "continuous" Pokémon Power, so it never needs to be announced. (It is always "on" unless Haunter is Asleep, Confused, or Paralyzed).
- Transparency only protects Haunter from attacks. Transparency does not protect Haunter from Poison damage, or damaged applied with Pokémon Powers (like Gengar's Curse, Alakazam's Damage Swap, and Machamp's Strikes Back).
- Transparency is turned off when Haunter is Confused, so it will not protect Haunter from self-inflicted damage resulting from a failed attack.
- Transparency will protect Haunter from attack damage while Haunter is either Active or Benched. (Bench damage from a Self-destructing Pokémon for example.)
- You are allowed only 4 total Haunter in your deck regardless of which expansion they come from. (You are not allowed to include 4 Basic Set Haunter and 4 Fossil Haunter in the same deck).

STRATEGY:

- You should now feel free to throw away every copy of "Basic" set Haunter (level 22) you own! Fossil Haunter is absolutely superior in every aspect of game play. No Weakness! No Retreat Cost! Half the time, your opponent's attacks (no matter how devastating) will do absolutely nothing to Haunter! Of course offense is not Haunter's strong point, but that's what Gengar was printed for. This is one evolution line that doesn't need a Pokémon Breeder!

HITMONLEE (LV30)
CARD: 7 (Holo) + 22/62
RATING: 4
RULINGS:
- Hitmonlee's Trainer gets to choose which benched Pokémon to apply Stretch Kick's damage to.
- Stretch Kick will not inflict damage to the Active Pokémon (even if the defender does not have any benched Pokémon.)
- Stretch Kick does not inflict damage to the "Defender" (your opponent's Active Pokémon), so a PlusPower attached to Hitmonlee when using Stretch Kick will have no effect.

STRATEGY:
- Is the Fossil expansion just the coolest set of cards ever printed or what?!?! Hitmonlee is so incredibly disruptive to use against opponents. Although there are other Pokémon that can inflict damage to benched Pokémon, most of them affect your own Pokémon as badly as the opponents. And none of them are as selective, or do as much damage as Stretch Kick.
- High Jump Kick is nearly the most efficient attack move of any Basic Pokémon. Typically a monster must evolve to a Stage 2 or Stage 1 before being able to inflict 50 damage for only 3 energy.

COMBOS:
- Hitmonlee + Gust of Wind: Keep your opponent's most expensive retreater up front using Gust of Wind cards, while Hitmonlee concentrates on taking out their offensive threats stuck on the bench using Stretch Kick.

HORSEA (LV19)
CARD: 49/62
RATING: 3
RULINGS:
- Smokescreen's effect (requiring the defending Pokémon to flip a coin prior to attacking) will remain for one turn with the defender even after Horsea is benched. This effect resides with the defender, and will only go away if the defender is Benched or Evolved.

STRATEGY:
- A zero Retreat Cost is an extreme advantage in the Pokémon TCG. With so many status effects in the game that can affect your Pokémon (like Poison, Confusion, Smokescreen, etc.), the ability to retreat without a discard can be a life saver. Remember that all status effects that reside with a Pokémon are removed when that Pokémon is Benched or Evolved.
- Smokescreen is definitely an attack move that is weighted in favor of Horsea. For only 1 Water energy, Horsea will inflict 10 damage and attach a negative status effect to the Defender. Not even a Gust of Wind on your Horsea will allow your opponent to attack with their Smokescreened attacker without first passing a coin flip.

HYPNO (LV36)
CARD: 8 (Holo) + 23/62
RATING: 2
RULINGS:
- Just like Pokédex, Hypno's Prophecy attack does not allow you to discard the cards drawn or allow you to shuffle your deck after replacing them. You are only allowed to rearrange the cards drawn before placing them back on top of the deck they were drawn from.

STRATEGY:
- Hypno is the long awaited evolution to Drowzee from the Basic set of TCG cards. Neither card is truly overwhelming to your opponents, but both offer decent stamina and interesting attack moves.
- Hypno's Dark Mind attack move seems slightly expensive at 3 Psychic energy for 40 total damage. But the ability to attack two creatures at once, and decent Hit Points make Hypno a definite candidate as "filler" in any mono-Psychic manipulation deck.

COMBOS:
- Hypno + Moltres: Use Hypno's Prophecy attack move to position your opponent's worst card on top of their deck. Once they have drawn this card, you can now retreat Hypno to advance Moltres and Wildfire the best 2 cards into their discard pile.

KABUTO (LV09)
CARD: 50/62
RATING: 2
RULINGS:
- Kabuto Armor is a "continuous" Pokémon Power, so it never needs to be announced. (It is always "on" unless Kabuto is Asleep, Confused, or Paralyzed).
- Kabuto Armor only protects Kabuto from attacks. Kabuto Armor does not protect Kabuto from Poison damage, or damaged applied with Pokémon Powers (like Gengar's Curse, Alakazam's Damage Swap, and Machamp's Strikes Back).
- Kabuto Armor is turned off when Kabuto is Confused, so it will not protect Kabuto from self-inflicted damage resulting from a failed attack.
- If an attack normally inflicts 10 damage, Kabuto Armor will convert this to 0 damage.
- Kabuto Armor will protect Kabuto from attack damage while Kabuto is either Active or Benched. (Bench damage from a Self-destructing Pokémon for example.)

COMBOS:
- Kabuto + Articuno: Used as a guarantee that your fighting Articuno has a replacement in case it is knocked-out, Kabuto Armor will completely block all damage from a failed coin flip during Articuno's Blizzard attack move. Of course you will never really want to attack with Kabuto, so having a few on your bench is not that much of an advantage!

KABUTOPS (LV30)
CARD: 9 (Holo) + 24/62
RATING: 2
RULINGS:

- When Kabutops attacks a Pokémon with Resistance to Fighting, Absorb will typically yield only 10 damage onto the opponent. In this case, Absorb removes 10 damage from Kabutops (since half of 10 is 5, which rounds up to 10).

STRATEGY:

- Kabutops is the disappointing pinnacle to a disappointing evolution line of monsters. With virtually every color in the game providing at least some Resistance to Fighting (most Pokémon birds are Fighting Resistant), Fighting type Pokémon like Kabutops need to be faster, healthier, and more powerful than all the rest. Kabutops is none of these things. It is a 2nd Stage monster (slow) with only 60 HP (sick) and very expensive attacks (weak)! Cool art and holographic foil can only take a card so far...

COMBOS:

- Kabutops + a good book: Since this Shellfish Pokémon can't handle battle, it might make a decent bookmark!.

KINGLER (LV27)
CARD: 38/62
RATING: 1
RULINGS:

- If there are zero damage counters on Kingler, then Flail will do zero damage.

STRATEGY:

- Flail is the epitome of a double-edged sword. In order to be a substantial attack move, Kingler needs to have significant damage on itself. Unfortunately that severely limits the number of rounds that Kingler will be dishing out efficient Flail attacks.
- The best attack plan for a reliable deck that includes Kingler would be to power up Crabhammer as soon as possible. Hopefully you can get a round or two of 40 damage attacks off before Kingler's Flail starts looking like the more damaging offense.

COMBOS:

- Kingler + Self-destruction: Kingler is one of the few Pokémon that could possibly benefit from Self-destruction bench damage. After your Magneton Self-destructs, Kingler will immediately have damage counters to power up its mighty Flail of Frustration!.

KRABBY (LV20)
CARD: 51/62
RATING: 3
RULINGS:

- If there are no Krabby cards in your deck when using "Call for Family", this attack effectively does nothing, and you may not attack again until your next turn.

STRATEGY:

- Irongrip is somewhat appealing because of the partial colorless energy requirement. Many water Pokémon are strictly dependent on Water energy only, so Krabby will help in multi-color decks that want a little bit of Water included to douse all the Fire decks that may be running rampant in their area.
- A retreat cost of 2 for a relatively small basic Pokémon like this is pretty large. Be sure to include Switch or Scoop Up trainer cards to offset this disadvantage and get Krabby out of harm's way.

COMBOS: Krabby + Wigglytuff: After using Krabby to fill your bench with monsters using Call for Family, you can retreat in favor of a (now) heavy hitting Wigglytuff that will be "Doing the Wave" for up to 60 damage per turn.

SINGLE CARD RULES/STRATEGY

LAPRAS (LV31)
CARD: 10 (Holo) + 25/62
RATING: 4
RULINGS:
- Lapras' Water Gun will do 10 damage if there is one Water Energy attached, 20 damage with two Water Energy attached, or 30 damage with three Water Energy attached. Water Energy attached beyond the third does not increase damage dealt.

STRATEGY:
- For a nearly extinct wild Pokémon, Lapras sure can put up a fight! 80 HP is phenomenal for a Basic Pokémon, and Confuse Ray is always the right strategy to employ against other high-HP monsters. Once your opponent is safely confused (and they are afraid to attack or retreat), Lapras should make efficient use of its Water Gun attack move for optimal damage dealing.
- Water Gun moves are outstanding attacks for use while your Pokémon is still accumulating energy cards. Instead of forcing you to wait until you have satisfied some large energy cost to use a powerful attack, Water Gun will grow with your Pokémon. As your monster's energy grows, so will this attack!

MAGMAR (LV31)
CARD: 39/62
RATING: 5
RULINGS:
- Smokescreen's effect (requiring the defending Pokémon to flip a coin prior to attacking) will remain for one turn with the defender even after Magmar is benched. This effect resides with the defender, and will only go away if the defender is Benched, or Evolved.
- You are allowed only 4 total Magmar in your deck regardless of which expansion they come from. (You are not allowed to include 4 Basic Set Magmar and 4 Fossil Magmar in the same deck).

STRATEGY:
- Although Basic set's version of Magmar was not a bad TCG card, Fossil Magmar works much better in nearly all Fire decks. Smokescreen's 1 energy requirement gives Magmar the capability to attack starting in round #1. All Fire decks should typically strive to attack fast! And Fossil Magmar's increased Hit Points also allow it to stay in battle longer and punish its opponents more!
- As soon as possible start using Magmar's Smog attack against new defenders. Once successfully poisoned, you may want to revert back to attacking with Smokescreen. While the opponent is accruing Poison damage every turn, 50% of their counter-attacks will be nullified with Smokescreen's effect.

MAGNETON (LV35)
CARD: 11 (Holo) + 26/62
RATING: 2
RULINGS:
- Each Defender trainer card attached to Magneton will subtract an additional 20 damage. It is possible to keep Magneton from knocking itself out after its own Self-destruct with enough Defender trainer cards attached.
- You are allowed only 4 total Magneton in your deck regardless of which expansion they come from. (You are not allowed to include 4 Basic Set Magneton and 4 Fossil Magneton in the same deck).

STRATEGY:
- As with the Basic set version of Magneton, the best strategy for the Pokémon player to follow when getting Fossil Magneton in a booster pack is to trade it away as soon as possible.
- Sonicboom would be underpowered even against normally weak Pokémon, but it doesn't even allow this unlikely benefit. If there were more Pokémon cards (other than a few Fighting type monsters) that Sonicboom could sneak under a normal Resistance to Lightning, this attack may serve a purpose in mono-Lightning decks. A better solution for the mono-Lightning player however, would be to utilize other colored (or colorless) attackers in their decks.

MOLTRES (LV35)
CARD: 12 (Holo) + 27/62
RATING: 5
RULINGS:
- Moltres is allowed to discard the last remaining Fire energy attached to Moltres (when using its Wildfire attack move) in order to discard another card from the opponent's deck.
- Discarding Fire energy with Moltres' Wildfire attack move is not a cost, so a Metronome copy of this attack would still require Clefairy/Clefable to discard Fire energy cards in order to use it. (A "cost" is anything that must be satisfied in order for the attack to be used. Since Wildfire can be used without discarding any Fire energy, this discard is not a cost, and therefore copied by Metronome.)

STRATEGY:
- Dive Bomb is not for the feint of heart! With only 50% chance of all that Fire energy being useful, only a brave Pokémon Trainer will rely on this monster to register a few K-O's. Don't feel too badly for Moltres Masters however, all of that Fire energy will hardly be wasted if they remember to Wildfire it away before Moltres is K-O'd and sent to the discard pile. Remember, a Pokémon TCG player loses the game if they have no cards left in their draw pile at the start of their turn. This is exactly what Wildfire was designed to expedite!

MUK (LV34)
CARD: 13 (Holo) + 28/62
RATING: 5
RULINGS:

- Toxic Gas is a "continuous" Pokémon Power, so it never needs to be announced. (It is always "on" unless Muk is Asleep, Confused, or Paralyzed).
- Toxic Gas specifically does not affect other Toxic Gasses. With multiple copies of Muk in play, all of them will have Toxic Gas in effect. (They do not cancel each other out.)
- Toxic Gas cannot be turned "off" unless Muk is Asleep, Confused, or Paralyzed.
- Toxic Gas affects Muk's Trainer's other Pokémon as well as Muk's opponent's Pokémon.

STRATEGY:

- Grass certainly has better attackers to rely on for applying pressure to the opponent. However, nothing is better at shutting down your opponent's nasty Pokémon Power combinations than a Muk in play. Best used in heavy-hitting, straightforward attack decks, leave Muk on your bench and attack without fear of silly mimes and their Invisible Walls, or crazy turtles and their ability to Rain Dance on your parade!

OMANYTE (LV19)
CARD: 52/62 • **RATING:** 4
RULINGS:

- Clairvoyance is a "continuous" Pokémon Power, so it never needs to be announced. (It is always "on" unless Omanyte is Asleep, Confused, or Paralyzed).
- Clairvoyance will force Omanyte's opponent to play with his or her hand face up while Omanyte is either Active or Benched.
- Omanyte's Water Gun will do 10 damage if there is one Water Energy attached, 20 damage with two Water Energy attached, or 30 damage with three Water Energy attached. Water Energy attached beyond the third does not increase damage dealt.

STRATEGY:

- Water Gun moves are outstanding attacks for use while your Pokémon is still accumulating energy cards. Instead of forcing you to wait until you have satisfied some large energy cost to use a powerful attack, Water Gun will grow with your Pokémon. As your monster's energy grows, so will this attack!
- Omanyte is best utilized on your bench however. It should stay relatively safe there, and Clairvoyance will give you total visibility of all aspects of your opponent's game plan. Because there is so little for a player to do during their opponent's turn in the Pokémon TCG, it is imperative for players to "plan ahead" and try to anticipate an opponent's moves. Clairvoyance will allow you to choose the optimal attack strategy and give you all the information you need to avoid your opponent's strategies.

COMBOS: Omanyte + Impostor Professor Oak: Rather than playing Impostor Oak and hoping that you have hurt their position, why not put out an Omanyte first and guarantee that you will use the Impostor at an appropriate time!

OMASTAR (LV32)
CARD: 40/62
RATING: 1
RULINGS:
- Omastar's Water Gun will do 20 damage if there is two Water Energy attached, 30 damage with three Water Energy attached, or 40 damage with four Water Energy attached. Water Energy attached beyond the fourth does not increase damage dealt.
- If you flip two tails using Spike Cannon, then this attack will do zero damage.

STRATEGY:
- Aaaah! Run away! The artwork isn't the only thing creepy with this Pokémon card! Expending the effort to evolve Mysterious Fossil all the way up to Omastar will not impress your opponent. In fact, wasting this much time and effort for a 70 HP monster with a minor Water Gun attack may only make your opponent feel sorry for you.

STRATEGY:
- Headache is just delaying the inevitable. Since Psyduck cannot dispatch defenders using Headache, there is little or no benefit to using this attack move. If you suspect your opponent is holding a bunch of Energy Removal cards for you, Headache will just ensure that they get the chance to draw a few more before you allow them to play.
- Fury Swipes will average out to 50% of 30 damage per turn (or 15 average damage per turn). If you trust the law of averages, this is slightly better than all those 10 damage first turn attacks. Of course there are other Pokémon (and Water Pokémon) that have better first turn attacks that do not rely on averages.

PSYDUCK (LV15)
CARD: 53/62
RATING: 3
RULINGS:
- Question: If Psyduck uses Headache, can Psyduck's opponent play Mysterious Fossil or Clefairy Doll (Trainer cards that count as Pokémon while in play)?
- Answer: Mysterious Fossil and Clefairy Doll are Trainer cards while in your hand, and while "being played" to the table. However, they are special Trainer cards that may be played at any time a Basic Pokémon card may be played (at game setup for example). Once they are in-play on the table, they are no longer considered Trainer cards, but Pokémon cards. But, Headache's effect prevents Trainer cards from "being played", so it will prevent Psyduck's opponent from playing Mysterious Fossil and Clefairy Doll (since they remain Trainer cards until actually in-play on the table).

COMBOS:
- Psyduck + Lass: If Psyduck isn't in immediate danger from fainting, try using Headache for several consecutive rounds. Once you are sure that your opponent has accrued a healthy quantity of trainer cards, just Lass them all back into their decks and make them draw them again before using them!.

RAICHU (LV45)
CARD: 14 (Holo) + 29/62
RATING: 4
RULINGS:
- Raichu's owner (not Raichu's opponent) chooses which benched Pokémon will be damaged with Gigashock's bench damage.
- Gigashock inflicts 10 damage to benched Pokémon, regardless of whether there are fewer than 3 Pokémon on your opponent's bench. For example: If your opponent has only 1 benched Pokémon when you successfully use Gigashock, do 10 damage to this Pokémon. The remaining damage capability of Gigashock is wasted (just as if your opponent had no benched monsters).
- You are allowed only 4 total Raichu in your deck regardless of which expansion they come from. (You are not allowed to include 4 Basic Set Raichu and 4 Fossil Raichu in the same deck).

STRATEGY:
- Although Fossil Raichu is a much better Pokémon to attack with than Basic set's version of this monster, the four Lightning energy requirement for Gigashock will severely slow down how quickly Raichu can be called upon during battle.
- Always be wary of using Fighting Weakness Lightning Pokémon (like Fossil Raichu) when Fighting heavy hitting decks are so popular. Raichu's 90 HP will shrink amazingly fast against an efficient Fighting machine!

SANDSLASH (LV33)
CARD: 41/62
RATING: 3
RULINGS:
- If you flip three tails using Fury Swipes, then this attack will do zero damage.

STRATEGY:
- Both Sandshrew (from the Basic Set) and Sandslash are average attackers. The colorless energy requirement for Slash is misplaced on an evolution card that has a Basic Pokémon with no colorless energy requirements. However, colorless attacks are always desirable to competitive players who seek to build multi-functional tournament decks. And this is where Sandslash really shines. As a rock type Pokémon it is one of the few cards in the game with Resistance to Lightning. The Fossil expansion has boosted Lightning attack prowess significantly, and Sandslash's Resistance can be the key factor in many Pokémon matches.

SEADRA (LV23)
CARD: 42/62
RATING: 3
RULINGS:

- Seadra's Water Gun will do 20 damage if there is two Water Energy attached, 30 damage with three Water Energy attached, or 40 damage with four Water Energy attached. Water Energy attached beyond the fourth does not increase damage dealt.
- A successful Agility does not stop your opponent from attacking. It merely prevents all damage and effects from affecting Seadra.
- Agility's effect is shut off if Seadra is benched, or devolved.
- Agility's effect is not shut off if the opponent benches his/her Pokémon that was damage by the successful Agility. (Only benching Seadra will disable this effect.)

STRATEGY:

- Agility is a highly underrated Attack Move and very easy for Seadra's Trainer to power with the Colorless energy requirements. After a successful coin toss, your opponent will be helpless to do much of anything except twiddle her thumbs, waiting for your next attack.

SHELLDER (LV08)
CARD: 54/62
RATING: 2
RULINGS:

- A successful Hide in Shell does not stop your opponent from attacking. It merely prevents all damage from being applied Shellder.
- Hide in Shell's effect is shut off if Shellder is benched or evolved.
- Hide in Shell's effect is not shut off if the opponent benches his/her Pokémon that was attacked by the successful Hide in Shell. (Only benching Shellder will disable this effect.)

STRATEGY:

- Hide in Shell is the exact same template as used for Chansey's Scrunch attack move. Scrunch is a staple in nearly all heavy evolution or stall decks. It provides the evolution trainer the time needed to get their deck rolling, and their attackers ready to go. Hide in Shell is *not* Scrunch, and Shellder is *definitely not* Chansey however. With only 30 Hit Points, a failed Hide in Shell is disaster for Shellder. (Chansey's 120 Hit Points allow it plenty of rounds to give up with failed Scrunches.)
- Supersonic is the only saving grace for Shellder. It is one of the few cards in the game that can Confuse the opponent as early as turn #1, and confusion will generally slow an opponent down just as much as a whole series of successful Hide in Shell moves. Be sure not to waste your attack with additional Supersonic moves if your opponent is already Confused—use Hide in Shell at that point.

SLOWBRO (LV26)
CARD: 43/62
RATING: 4
RULINGS:

- Damage moved onto Slowbro by the Strange Behavior Pokémon Power is not damage from an "attack" and therefore a Defender trainer card will not protect Slowbro from this damage.

STRATEGY:

- Slowbro has pretty low hit points for a 1st Stage evolution Pokémon, but Psyshock is a pretty fun attack move to use. For 2 Psychic energy, Slowbro can inflict 20 damage (40 if the defender is weak to Psychic) and has a decent chance to Paralyze the opponent as well. With enough rounds of Paralyzing your opponent with Psyshock, 20 damage is more than adequate to get the job done.

- By far, however, Slowbro's most powerful ability is its Strange Behavior Pokémon Power. Keep Slowbro safe on your bench where it (and possibly a few neighboring Slowbros) can soak up damage counters off of your more offensive attackers like Kadabra or Jynx. Once Slowbro can't take any more damage, use a Scoop Up or Mr. Fuji to get Slowbro safely out of play and deny your opponent their prize.

COMBOS:

- Slowbro + Mr. Fuji: Fill Slowbro up with as many damage counters as it can hold, then erase it all in one turn with a Mr. Fuji trainer card. And since Mr. Fuji puts Slowbro back into your deck, you have the opportunity to make use of Slowbro for a damage soak later in the game as well!

SLOWPOKE (LV18)
CARD: 55/62
RATING: 4
RULINGS:

- When printed on a card, "damage counter" means the same thing as "10 damage". Regardless of how many damage each glass bead you use represents, a successful Spacing Out will only remove 10 damage from Slowpoké.

- Since Slowpoké has Weakness to Psychic (its own type), a confused Slowpoké that fails the coin flip when attempting to attack will attack itself for 40 damage. This is double the normal 20 damage due to Slowpoké's Weakness.

STRATEGY:

- Who said that attacking in the Pokémon TCG needs to be all about damage? Both of Slowpoké's attack moves lack direct damage to the opponent, however they do provide strategic elements that are key in many powerful card combinations. Scavenge is especially potent in stall decks utilizing Energy Removal trainer cards to keep the opponent from developing their attackers.

COMBOS:

- Slowpoké + Energy Removal: In Pokémon, all players are limited to playing a single energy card per turn. Playing a simple Energy Removal trainer card can wipe out your opponent's entire turn of energy allocation without losing a single other card in play (except for the Energy Removal card itself). With a deck consisting of Slowpokés, Energy Removals, and a whole lot of Psychic Energy cards, you can Energy Removal your opponent EVERY turn and use Scavenge to pull it back into your hand for the next round. If your opponent can't put up a fight with their dwindling energy supply they will eventually run out of cards and lose the game.

TENTACOOL (LV10)
CARD: 56/62
RATING: 2
RULINGS:
- Just as it says on the card, Tentacool may not use Cowardice (to return to your hand) during the same turn that you put Tentacool into play.

STRATEGY:
- Cowardice is like having a built in Scoop Up (and always exactly when you need it too!) Of course when Tentacool only has 30 Hit Points to stash damage counters on, this power will be of limited use against all but the weakest of attackers.

COMBOS:
- Tentacool + Alakazam: Use Alakazam to move 20 damage off of your Active Pokémon and onto Tentacool waiting on your bench. Now, before your attack, you can Cowardice Tentacool back to your hand (and remove the 20 damage from the game). Replay Tentacool to your bench so that he is capable of soaking up 20 damage and turning tail again on your next turn! With an Alakazam and four Tentacools on your bench, your Active Pokémon would be able to free itself of 80 damage every turn and remain nearly invincible.

TENTACRUEL (LV21)
CARD: 44/62
RATING: 3
STRATEGY:
- Tentacruel's TCG card is true to form with the cartoon series and Game Boy games. It's a real "gangster of the sea". It strikes without warning and can leave your opponents dazed and confused. Be sure to make use of Tentacruel's free retreat cost for an easy getaway after successfully Confusing or Poisoning the defending monster. There is nothing better at disrupting your opponent's "game plan" than confusing their Active Pokémon. Once inflicted, they will be torn between wasting energy on a possible failed retreat attempt, or even worse: accidentally attacking themselves!

COMBOS:
- Tentacruel + Gust of Wind: Play Gust of Wind to force one of your opponent's high retreat-cost or undeveloped Pokémon to the active position. Then confuse or poison it with Tentacruel's status ailment attack moves. This is a great strategy to use against Pokémon TCG trainers that leave a few too many unprepared monsters on their bench. And remember that a confused Pokémon will no longer be able to use its Pokémon Powers—Tentacruel can teach all those annoying decks that rely on strong Pokémon Powers a thing or two!

WEEZING (LV27)
CARD: 45/62
RATING: 2
RULINGS:

- Each Defender trainer card attached to Weezing will subtract an additional 20 damage. It is possible to keep Weezing from knocking itself out from its own Self-destruct with enough Defender trainer cards attached.

STRATEGY:

- Many competitive players found out early how useful Base set Koffing can be. Poison and Confusion are the two best status effects in the game to inflict on your opponent, and Koffing has the opportunity to do both! The only major limitation with Koffing was the low base damage that Foul Gas deals.
- Weezing adds a finishing touch onto Koffing's longevity as an attacker with its Self-destruct attack move. Rarely will a player want to play Weezing until Koffing's number is up. Foul Gas can be so much more effective at eliminating a defender's threat than Weezing's Smog attack move. But, when it's clear that Koffing will be going down on your opponent's next turn, evolve into Weezing and Self-destruct for a glorious finale!

COMBOS:

- Weezing + Gust of Wind: Rather than waste all 60 Self-destruct damage on an opposing Pokémon that requires only 10 more damage to K-O, use Gust of Wind to bring up one of your opponent's less damaged monsters. With the bench damage inflicted by Self-destruct, you will still get the K-O against the weak Pokémon sent back to the bench, and you might even take out the gusted monster as well!

ZAPDOS (LV40)
CARD: 15 (Holo) + 30/62
RATING: 4
RULINGS:

- The luck of the coin toss must decide which benched Pokémon are damaged with Thunderstorm. Choose each Pokémon before flipping the coin for it, to ensure that neither player can selectively apply damage to benched monsters.
- You are allowed only 4 total Zapdos in your deck regardless of which expansion they come from. (You are not allowed to include 4 Basic Set Zapdos and 4 Fossil Zapdos in the same deck).

STRATEGY:

- Can you say "160 damage?" Can you say "Nasty!" Zapdos has immense potential with its awesome Thunderstorm attack. Because of the time that four Lighting energy requires, it will be hard to surprise your opponent with Zapdos. But if you wait to play this monster until after their bench is already full, there will be little that they can do to reduce the number of Thunderstorm targets!

COMBOS:

- Zapdos + Defender: Remember that Defender will not only protect your Pokémon from your opponent's attacks during their turn, it can also protect your Pokémon from self-inflicted damage during the turn it is played. Right before attacking with a massive Thunderstorm, be sure to play Defender on Zapdos to reduce up to 20 self-inflicted damage done by any unlucky coin flips.

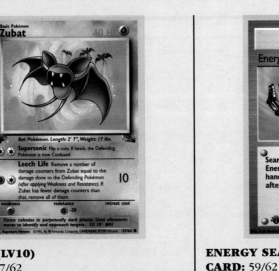

ZUBAT (LV10)
CARD: 57/62
RATING: 4
RULINGS:
- Since Pokémon can never be Confused and Asleep at the same time, a successful Supersonic attack will wake up a sleeping Pokémon in order to confuse it.
- Leech Life only counts damage that was actually applied to the defender. So damage that was cut out due to Resistance or a Defender trainer card must not be included in Leech Life's healing ability.
- Leech Life will remove damage from Zubat equal to all damage inflicted, even if less than this total damage was required to knock out the defending Pokémon. (The defender may only need 10 more damage to be K-O'd, but after weakness Leech Life might inflict 20 damage and Zubat gets to subtract all of that from itself.)

STRATEGY:
- Zubat has everything going to make it a highly useful Pokémon. The mostly Colorless attack requirements ensure that Zubat works well in multi-colored decks where the number of Grass energy cards is significantly reduced. The resistance to Fighting is always advantageous considering the number of hard hitting Haymaker decks running amok in the tournament scene. Lastly, its zero retreat cost makes Zubat highly mobile and able to flee to the safety of your bench after successfully confusing the opponent's active Pokémon with Supersonic. With only 10 more Hit Points (up to 50 from its 40), Zubat would be classed among some of the best Basic Pokémon in the game.

ENERGY SEARCH
CARD: 59/62
RATING: 4
RULINGS:
- Energy Search cannot be used to pull a Double Colorless Energy card from your draw pile since it is not a Basic Energy card.
- You must show your opponent the Basic Energy card that you removed from your draw pile after using Energy Search. This eliminates the temptation to use Energy Search to pull something other than an energy card in critical situations.

STRATEGY:
- Energy Search is a perfectly balanced card. The obvious advantage of being able to pull exactly the correct color of energy card in a multi-colored deck is offset by the negative effect of wasting a slot in your deck for a trainer card instead of an energy card. Every use of Energy Search is eating 2 cards out of your draw pile (1 for drawing Energy Search and 1 for the extracted Basic Energy card). Of course, in highly tuned offensive decks, the ability to eat through more of your draw pile in a short period of time can be as much of an advantage as it is disadvantage.

GAMBLER
CARD: 60/62

RATING: 3

RULINGS:

- If your deck has fewer cards in it then you are required to draw with Gambler, simply draw all remaining cards. You only lose the game if you cannot draw a card at the beginning of your turn, not if you cannot draw all cards that a card tells you to draw.
- "Shuffle your hand into your deck" does not require that you have any cards left in your hand. It only requires you to shuffle any cards you *may* have in your hand prior to drawing new cards. Therefore you may use Gambler if it is the last remaining card in your hand.

STRATEGY:

- Gambler is always best utilized when your hand is nearly depleted of cards. Since there is a 50% opportunity of drawing only 1 new card after returning your hand to your deck, minimize your disadvantage by making sure that any cards you do shuffle back into your deck are few and not currently useful.

COMBOS:

- Gambler + Evolution cards: The problem with evolution cards (especially 2nd Stage evolutions) is the order in which they *must* be played. Many times a player will find themselves with the evolution card before drawing the Basic Pokémon card. Use Gambler's ability to shuffle these premature cards back into your deck before drawing additional cards from the draw pile. (Preferably you get to draw 8 new cards, but even 1 new card is more useful than an evolution card that can't be played).

MR. FUJI
CARD: 58/62

RATING: 4

STRATEGY:

- Mr. Fuji's ability to move the removed Pokémon back into your deck (instead of the discard pile) is a huge advantage. And the fact that you get to shuffle all of the evolution and energy cards back into your deck as well is just phenomenal. However, unlike the Scoop Up rare trainer card from the base set, Mr. Fuji will only work on benched Pokémon. This is a pretty big limitation, and keeps Mr. Fuji's usefulness limited to very specialized situations. Since your Active Pokémon is receiving all of the damage and status effects from the opponent, it is usually your Active Pokémon that you need to remove from play. Unless you have a Pokémon with a free retreat cost (and isn't paralyzed, confused, or asleep), using Mr. Fuji will first require retreating. While play testing with Mr. Fuji in your deck, keep track of how many instances you would have preferred having a Scoop Up instead of the Mr. Fuji you were holding so that you can fine tune your ratio between these two awesome trainer cards.

COMBOS: Mr. Fuji + Alakazam: The Mr. Fuji trainer card was obviously designed with a single type of deck in mind: A Damage Swap deck that utilizes an Alakazam and big Hit Point Pokémon on your bench to keep the active attacker in battle as long as possible. In combination with Pokémon Centers to wipe the benched damage soakers clean of damage, Mr. Fuji can further support this theme and extend the depth of your draw pile at the same time. Many Damage Swap decks rely on "decking" the opponent to secure the win, and Mr. Fuji fits right in with that goal.

MYSTERIOUS FOSSIL
CARD: 62/62
RATING: 3
RULINGS:

- Mysterious Fossil and Clefairy Doll are Trainer cards while in your hand, in your discard pile, in your deck, and while BEING played to the table. Therefore:

  a) Psyduck's Headache effect will prevent you from playing Mysterious Fossil during your next turn.

  b) Mysterious Fossil may be retrieved from the discard pile with Item Finder.

  c) You may not use Mysterious Fossil with Pokémon Trader (either out of your hand or your deck).

  d) Mysterious Fossil does *not* count as a Basic Pokémon card in your hand when you are checking for a mulligan at the beginning of the game (you must still have a Basic Pokémon card in your hand in order to not have a mulligan.)

- However, they are special Trainer cards that may be played at any time a Basic Pokémon card may be played. Therefore you may play Mysterious Fossil or Clefairy Doll at game setup as one of your first Pokémon on the table.

- Once they are in-play on the table, Mysterious Fossil and Clefairy Doll are no longer considered Trainer cards, but Pokémon cards. Therefore:

  a) You may use Pokémon Breeder to evolve Fossil into Kabutops or Omastar.

  b) You may also devolve back into Mysterious Fossil using Devolution Spray.

  c) You may play energy cards onto Mysterious Fossil or Clefairy Doll.

  d) You may not evolve Mysterious Fossil during the same turn that it is put into play.

COMBOS:

- Mysterious Fossil + Devolution Spray: One of Mysterious Fossil's most powerful features is the lack of prize card that your opponent gets after knocking

RECYCLE
CARD: 61/62
RATING: 3
STRATEGY:

- Recycle is currently the only card in the Pokémon Trading Card Game that allows the retrieval of Pokémon cards out of your discard pile. Item Finder is very specifically limited to trainer cards, and Energy Retrieval can only fetch Basic Energy cards. In order to maintain effective evolution card ratios, there will typically be very few of these cards in your deck. Use Recycle to get them back into play if they end up in your discard pile.

COMBOS:

- Recycle + Bill: Bill is an extremely powerful trainer card that should be included in most competitive Pokémon decks already. When combined with a successful Recycle coin flip, Bill and Recycle can replace Item Finder with a bonus: no "wasted" cards. Item Finder requires the discard of Item Finder itself plus 2 additional cards in order to obtain 1 trainer card from your discard pile. When Recycle works followed quickly by Bill, you are trading 2 cards from your hand in order to pull 2 new cards (one of which is *exactly* what you want out of your discard pile) from your deck!

it out. With only 10 Hit Points, that doesn't take up much time however. But, with Mysterious Fossil evolved into Aerodactyl or one of its other harder-to-faint Pokémon, it can stay in play longer and handle more damage. But, once that Pokémon's play time is about to be cut short by your opponent's next round of attack, you can devolve it back to Mysterious Fossil. The resulting K-O on Fossil does not yield a prize for your opponent.

TOURNAMENT WINNING DECKS II

The Pokémon Trading Card Game is great fun to play, but building your own personalized deck can be a little overwhelming at first. Luckily, we've tried to make this process a lot easier on you. This chapter includes full listings for ten original deck creations custom tooled by some of the game's brightest deck designers. And accompanying each and every deck is an in-depth analysis that should help you play them to their fullest!

One of the greatest features of the Pokémon TCG is that every deck has both strengths and weaknesses. Although there is typically a large disparage between a tournament viable deck and what you might find in a pre-constructed Theme deck, there is very little difference in overall balance and power among the various elite deck designs that consistently win at tournaments. Tournament champion Pokémon TCG decks do not suffer from grossly overpowered archetypes that stifle original design and competition. In the end, it should always be a matter of highest-level skill that decides a Pokémon duel. Each of the decks and strategies that fill these pages should help take you to that level.

All beginning Pokémon Trainers will appreciate these pre-made decks for the ability to focus on learning how to play a good, strategic game without worrying about designing their own tournament-worthy, competitive deck. This chapter can be used as a springboard to bring newer players into the ranks of tournament champions with a minimum investment of time and cards. And in many situations, if a rare card can be replaced with something a little easier to find, this information will be described.

The deck classifications used in this chapter fall into three broad categories (Beat-Down, Evolution, and Stall) and generally describe a particular set of tactics that are employed while playing these decks. A complete and excellent description of these categories can be found in our previous strategy guide that specifically covers the Base and Jungle sets of Pokémon TCG cards. Needless to say, "Beat-Down" is a fighting machine, while "Evolution" tends to take time to develop into its most devastating attacks. And "Stall" is only happy after a long and boring game in which the opponent takes their final Draw Pile card before the "Stall" player does.

Established players may find several new ideas here to further refine their own creations. The strategy and advice offered in these pages are all established success stories. If a particular game play nuance can impact the outcome of your match, our Tournament Winning Decks section will clearly specify what to watch for, and what should be taken advantage of. Each deck strategy section is divided into 3 main sections: Concept, Tips for Playing, and Pitfalls. Concepts describe the deck's theme and overall goal while Tips for Playing will provide all the juicy details needed to get you to that goal. Pitfalls call special attention to particularly bad match-ups or easily made mistakes that will hamper the performance of the deck. All total it's a huge cache of "tech"!

After researching all the Fossil single-card strategies in this guide, along with Pokémon Deck-struction and Base/Jungle single-card strategies in our previous book (the "Pokémon Trading Card Game Player's Guide"), you should be more than prepared to handle these decks. Get out your damage counters and your best game coin! Jump into the arena and take no prisoners!

WOODWORTH

Class: Beat-Down Deck

Pokémon (17)
(4) Jigglypuff
(3) Wigglytuff
(4) Scyther
(3) Fossil Magmar
(3) Hitmonchan

Energy (23)
(10) Fighting Energy
(9) Fire Energy
(4) Double Colorless Energy

Trainers (20)
(4) Bill
(3) Professor Oak
(3) Computer Search
(2) Item Finder
(3) PlusPower
(3) Gust of Wind
(2) Super Energy Removal

CONCEPTS: Named for a Texan with a mean streak, "Woodworth" is a deck creation best described as a Turbo-Wigglytuff deck with just a touch of "Fossil Tech". Everything in here is capable of making your opponent sweat. The cards included that aren't used to mess with your opponent's side of the table are all designed to pull that kind of stuff out of your deck.

TIPS FOR PLAYING: "Woodworth" is all about Beat-Down and card advantage. Don't let up, ever, no matter what opponent you may be facing. Keep the cards flowing and keep the defenders reeling. Bill! Bill! Bill! And when you've used up all those cards, Professor Oak to keep the drive alive! Seriously, do not worry about decking yourself with this weapon—you'll collect your final Prize way before that ever happens!

A perfect first turn draw will see Hitmonchan with at least 2 PlusPower cards,

Jigglypuff, a few Scythers and a Professor Oak to keep the cards rolling. Wigglytuff can be fully powered with energy and bench support as early as turn 2 with this deck. And a 60 damage Do the Wave attack on turn 2 is exactly what you want to shoot for when playing it. Use Computer Search to pull an Oak to help make this happen. And if that doesn't work, Item Finder to do it again!

PITFALLS: There are some major holes in long term strategy here, but "Woodworth" shouldn't have to worry too much about the long term game. A slow start may be difficult to overcome, but Fossil Magmar adds a lot of nice status effects that can slightly stall the opponent until the right combination of cards come your way. In the end, Wigglytuff should be calling all the shots and laying waste to your opponent's ranks.

RECURSIVE SCAVENGER

Class: Stall Deck

Pokémon (14)
(3) Fossil Gastly
(4) Slowpoke
(4) Chansey
(3) Mr. Mime

Energy (24)
(24) Psychic Energy

Trainers (22)
(4) Gambler
(2) Bill
(3) Computer Search
(1) Impostor Professor Oak
(2) Scoop Up
(2) Recycle
(4) Pokémon Center
(4) Energy Removal

CONCEPTS: The purpose of "Recursive Scavenger" is to beat your opponent by forcing them to run out of cards. Like all good stalling decks, "Recursive Scavenger" doesn't waste time with offensive Pokémon. Everything piled into this deck is designed to "deck" your opponent: From Wall Pokémon like Mr. Mime and Chansey to defensive Trainer cards like Scoop Up and Pokémon Center. Even the normally offensive Energy Removals are included as part of a defensive strategy. This deck can get a little boring to play at times because every successful game will go to the very end of each player's deck. Preferably the opponent reaches the end of their deck before you!

TIPS FOR PLAYING: The biggest combo in this deck is Slowpoke + Energy Removal. If you're able to get Gastly out in front early and receive plenty of Psychic energy in your draws, you should be able to play Energy Removal every single turn and completely stall your opponent without energy for attacks. Play Energy Removal onto your opponent's active Pokémon, then use Slowpoke's Scavenge attack to retrieve the just-played Energy Removal card to your hand. You're all set for your next round of "attack"! Since your opponent is limited to only playing one energy card per turn, and this combo should allow you to play Energy Removal every turn, this can be a near guaranteed lock to stall your opponent out.

Gastly is included to make sure that your deck has plenty of energy cards to feed to Slowpoke's Scavenge attack. Use Gastly's Energy Conversion attack move when your relentless Energy Removal barrage has created a dead-spot in the game. Hopefully your opponent is without any energy cards in hand and is desperately drawing each turn looking for one. Keep restocking your hand with energy cards using Gastly until your opponent makes a move. Gastly may end up taking one for the team and fainting, but advance Slowpoke once again to keep the Energy Removal beat-down on.

Mr. Mime is included for its obvious stall benefits and not primarily for its attack. Invisible Wall can literally shut down some bigger decks without a small enough attack move to get under the Wall. This is best played later in the game after your opponent has already evolved into monsters with large attacks. Also included to support the recursive Energy Removal theme are a few Recycle trainer cards and Scoop Ups. A lucky coin flip and Recycle can yield the same result as Slowpoke's Scavenge, and Scoop Up will rescue a damaged Slowpoke, Chansey, or Mr. Mime from action.

Impostor Professor Oak is included and best used in a stall deck when the opponent's has very few cards in hand. Since Impostor Oak does not require them to discard their existing hand (it requires them to shuffle their hand into their deck instead), you can only use Impostor Oak to best advantage if they are holding fewer than 7 cards. The net effect if played correctly should be a decrease to the size of their draw pile. You are giving your opponent card advantage here, but "Recursive Scavenger's" Energy Removal game control should make that advantage negligible.

PITFALLS: Mono-Psychic decks can give "Recursive Scavenger" the most problems.

Slowpoke is the key monster in this deck and its weakness to Psychic can be a major thorn in your side. Even with playing Energy Removal every single turn, your opponent will always have at least one attack with one energy card available. Typically they will play one energy card onto their active Pokémon and attack. You definitely will be in a position to get rid of that energy card on your following turn, but if their attacker is a Psychic Pokémon with an attack requiring only one energy, double damage can put Slowpoke in the discard pile pretty quickly. Make sure that you make use of your Pokémon Centers and Scoop Ups to limit the number of Prize cards your opponent is able to take.

Rain Dance decks, when played correctly, can hurt just about every other deck in existence (including "Recursive Scavenger"). Luckily, most Rain Dance decks lack small attack moves and tend to use up all their energy in a few key turns. Use Mr. Mime to front against anything in a Rain Dance deck (like Blastoise, Dewgong, Gyarados, etc.) that can't get under the Invisible Wall, and use Chansey to stall against the few monsters that have smaller attacks (like an under-powered Lapras or a Seel). This would be an opportune time to use Chansey's Double-edge to remove these dangerous attackers with "small" moves from the game, so that Mr. Mime can get back in and guarantee zero damage from the bigger opponents.

FOSSILIZED RAIN DANCE

Class: Evolution Deck

Pokémon (16)
(4) Squirtle
(1) Wartortle
(4) Blastoise
(4) Articuno
(3) Lapras

Energy (22)
(22) Water Energy

Trainers (22)
(4) Professor Oak
(4) Bill
(3) Computer Search
(3) Item Finder
(3) Pokémon Breeder
(3) Gust of Wind
(2) Super Energy Removal

CONCEPTS: "Rain Dance" is a mono-Water Evolution Deck with a whole lot of firepower. The deck is chock full of heavy hitting monsters that can dish out damage like no other. The natural high-energy attack requirements of this deck's soldiers are balanced nicely by Blastoise's Rain Dance Pokémon Power. In fact, many players believe that Rain Dance is unbalanced, and unfair to use in tournaments. Don't let the frowns on the opposing player's faces deter you however. There can be only one Pokémon Master!

TIPS FOR PLAYING: This deck has a very simple goal: Get Blastoise out as soon as possible. Blastoise is critical to the all-important rush of attacks that will overrun the opponent. Rain Dance decks like this one sacrifice quite a bit in the quantity of monster cards department in order to rush into powerful attacks first. If the defending player has the time and opportunity

to develop some good opposition on their bench, you may not have the depth to handle their imminent onslaught.

With lots of Professor Oak, Computer Search, and Item Finder cards at your disposal, you should be looking at getting Blastoise into play as early as turn number 2. Pokémon Breeder makes this possible and is the preferred method of evolving your first Squirtle in play. There are so many duplicates to rely on in this deck construction, don't be afraid to Oak away a Blastoise or Pokémon Breeder in your hand if you lack that all-necessary Squirtle to get into play. Of course Computer Searching for a solitary missing link is probably the best tactic in that situation, but typically Search should be reserved for retrieving additional Professor Oaks to keep the Water energy cards flowing from your deck.

Rain Dance decks gained some great new cards to revitalize the archetype in the Fossil expansion. The best new additions from Fossil are Lapras and Articuno. They have key features that make them invaluable in this new class of Rain Dance deck. It's almost as if the original Pocket Monster Card Game designers felt sorry for what they did to hamper Rain Dance with the Jungle expansion. Scyther and Mr. Mime are both Jungle cards that together murdered Rain Dance's previously feared and respected role in the tournament environment.

Lapras is a basic Pokémon with relatively small attacks for this deck, but it should never be taken lightly. Both of Lapras' attack moves are vital to defeat Mr. Mime opposition. Mr. Mime's Invisible Wall has historically shut down Rain Dance decks unless they included status inducing or weak attackers (Lickitung was the classic retrofit). Water Gun has the nice feature of growing with additional development, and against a Psychic deck employing the Invisible Wall it can sneak under. Be sure to halt Lapras' supply of Water energy at 2 such that Water Gun is only inflicting 20 damage per round—the maximum that Mr. Mime will allow. And 2 Water energy is perfect for Confuse Ray, which happens to be a better defense against Pokémon Powers like Invisible Wall than Water Gun. Once confused, the Wall will turn "off" and Mr. Mime will be ripe for the fainting.

Articuno is the key attacker in this Fossilized Rain Dance deck. For a basic Pokémon with 70 Hit Points and two nasty attack moves, Articuno is a no-brainer for inclusion into any Water deck. And luckily for us, Rain Dance is just the thing that "Arti" needs to pump up in no time. Since most Pokémon that a Rain Dance player will have in play at any one time are extremely buff, don't worry too much about failed coin flips with Blizzard. The 50% of the time that your opponent's benched Pokémon are being hit by this damage will more than make up for a few extra damage counters on your own monsters. And, as always, when one hit with a 50-damage blizzard is not enough to take out the defending Pokémon, use Freeze Dry and try to paralyze them. This is especially useful in match ups with other Rain Dance decks.

PITFALLS: Rain Dance's historical pitfalls were plentiful, and the Fossil expansion just adds to the list. Fortunately Rain Dance is fast and brutal enough to bypass many of the Pokémon designed to short circuit it, and the new Water Pokémon from Fossil continue to shift power back to the Rain Dance player. The shift away from Gyarados in this Rain Dance deck makes it less susceptible to Scyther, and we already know how to deal with Mr. Mime.

This particular Rain Dance deck suffers badly to Lightning attacks. Be sure to use Lapras and Articuno's status effects (confusion and paralysis) on all yellow opponents. This will slow their approach and keep you in control of the match. Also, two new Pokémon from the Fossil expansion should be especially feared: Muk and Aerodactyl. If your opponent can get one of these Rain Dance "hosers" into play before Blastoise can work its magic, you may be done for. Use Gust of Wind and your meanest attacker (Articuno) to bring these monsters up front and take them down.

DEEP HAYMAKER

Class: Beat-Down Deck

Pokémon (17)
(4) Hitmonchan
(3) Hitmonlee
(4) Scyther
(3) Grimer
(3) Muk

Energy (22)
(11) Fighting Energy
(11) Grass Energy

Trainers (21)
(4) Bill
(2) Professor Oak
(3) Energy Removal
(3) Super Energy Removal
(3) Item Finder
(3) Gust of Wind
(3) PlusPower

CONCEPTS: "Haymaker" is the name of a speedy Fighting deck. The basic themes are fast, heavy attacks along with lots of Energy Removal. It is the epitome of "Beat-Down" decks. Strong basic Pokémon and low cost retreating are super important to this type of deck. Typically a Haymaker lacks the "depth" necessary to withstand late-game attackers, and compensates by never allowing the match to get that far. Evolved Pokémon typically contain powerful Pokémon Powers that can totally bypass a Haymaker's offense. This deck tries to give Haymaker some depth by adding Muk's Toxic Gas stranglehold on Pokémon Power combo decks.

TIPS FOR PLAYING: Hitmonchan and Hitmonlee are included primarily for offense. These are basic Pokémon with a lot of offensive potential. Nintendo knew what they were doing when they named these two Pokémon

after martial arts legends Jackie Chan and Bruce Lee. Scyther is included as Fighting resistance (to ward off your opponent's Hitmonchans and Hitmonlees) and for its free retreat cost. Slash is a little expensive for this deck—allocate most of your resources onto the "karate kids". Scyther's Swords Dance is a quaint little move that is useful about once only each game. Use it immediately prior to attaching the 3rd energy card for a 60 damage Slash. There is little point using Swords Dance beyond attaching the 3rd energy since two rounds of 30 damage is equal (and more difficult to defend against) than one round of 60.

Grimer is only included as a Muk foundation. Both of Grimer's attacks just scream out: "Attack me please!" You will be better off as the attacker in most cases. Muk's Toxic Gas is what it's all about. Even Sludge should be avoided as it is too slow for this deck's appetite. Keep Muk nice and safe on your bench where it will negate your opponent's Alakazam, Blastoise, Mr. Mime, and Venusaur combos. Muk is a little slow because it requires Grimer in play first, but most of the monsters Muk protects against will be even more slow in appearing.

There are 18 Pokémon cards in this deck and that significantly cuts into Haymaker's allocation of offensive Trainer cards. We've cut the Energy Removal and Super Energy Removal down to a total of 6 cards. Because of this, it will be imperative to monitor your opponent's progress and only use your ER cards where they provide the most disruption. Monsters with Double Colorless Energy cards attached or large retreat costs are always good targets for Energy Removal. Certainly never waste your Energy Removal cards on defenders that are about to be K-O'd.

PlusPower and Gust of Wind are included as "surprise" cards. Try to catch the opponent off-guard when you use these gems. PlusPower is remarkably useful during the early rounds of a match. Its great to see another player's face when a few PlusPower on a Hitmonchan dishes out 40 damage on turn #1. If you're extremely lucky, you'll get a Knock Out with it and perhaps even a Win if the opposing player is left without an in-play Pokémon. Even later in the game, PlusPower is most effective when played in multiples. Item Finder can retrieve extra copies from your discard pile if necessary.

Gust of Wind brings an added bonus in this particular deck. This trainer card is already extremely powerful, allowing you to select the best defender to beat on. But when combined with Hitmonlee's two attack moves, Gust of Wind makes for your opponent's worst nightmare. After a round or two of Stretch Kicks on the benched defender that you fear the most, use Gust of Wind to bring it up front where you can finish it off with a High Jump Kick. Keee-Yaaa! Or equally useful, use Gust of Wind to defeat your opponent's active Pokémon from their bench. Bring forward a Pokémon that you know cannot be easily retreated and then Stretch Kick the nasty defender while they are defenseless on the bench.

PITFALLS: Watch out for Fighting's standard weakness: Psychic opponents. Both Hitmonchan and Hitmonlee will be over their head quickly in that match-up. Even the lowly Grimer and Muk will cringe when they see a purple opponent. Scyther will be your best friend in these situations. We've included 4 copies of the Grass slasher just to make sure that one is always around when you need it.

Be careful to use your trainer cards wisely and choose targets that have the potential to create the most problems for this deck. Psychic Pokémon are always a threat and should be handled with hostility. However, Fighting resistant monsters (like Pokémon birds) will also be challenging to deal with, and represent acceptable targets for a timely Gust of Wind/Plus Power/Energy Removal.

PSYCHIC BUZZ

Class: Evolution Deck

Pokémon (21)
(4) Electabuzz
(4) Fossil Gastly
(3) Fossil Haunter
(2) Gengar
(3) Slowpoke
(2) Slowbro
(3) Mr. Mime

Energy (22)
(15) Psychic Energy
(7) Lightning Energy

Trainers (17)
(4) Bill
(3) Professor Oak
(2) Computer Search
(2) Energy Retrieval
(2) Scoop Up
(2) Gust of Wind
(2) Super Energy Removal

CONCEPTS: "Psychic Buzz" is really a multitude of offensive weapons hidden in a seemingly defensive deck. Electabuzz and Mr. Mime will be dishing out most of the punishment onto your opponents, while Slowbro and the Gengar line provide support. Psychic and Lightning seem to have so much synergy it's amazing that more combo decks featuring these two colors are not dominate in the tournament environment. The "Psychic Buzz" player should take advantage of this opening and make the most of their "metagame tech".

TIPS FOR PLAYING: "Damage Swap" decks are overpowering to nearly all opponents... once they get rolling. Up to the release of the Fossil expansion however, they were extremely slow to get up to speed. They all relied on Alakazam (a Stage 2 Pokémon) and it's manip-

ulative Pokémon Power. Alakazam can be incredibly slow to get into play unless the entire deck is designed around making this happen. Unfortunately that never seems to leave the TCG player with an offense that can make effective use of the Damage Swap safety cushion that they instigated with so much effort. Now that Fossil cards are available, we can consider using Slowbro's Strange Behavior as a reasonably suitable replacement for Damage Swap. And Slowbro's evolution is orders of magnitude easier to pull off in the heat of battle than Alakazam, making this a much more reliable feature.

Of course, as reliable as getting Slowbro into play may be, this deck isn't content to merely stall its way to victory. Both Slowbro and Slowpoke will serve useful in tight situations or occasional lapses of action. Slowpoke's

Pokémon TCG Fossil Expansion Player's Guide

Scavenge attack move is best used retrieving one of the card drawing trainers that present itself as the most appropriate for the circumstances. Professor Oak is typically the card of choice here, but on rare occasions Slowpoke may find an Energy Retrieval or Computer Search of more value. Pay close attention to the cards that have already passed through your hand and which are most likely to remain in your deck. It is impossible to determine this exactly without checking your prize pile, but just one Computer Search played and a full minute of browsing through your decks contents should make this information crystal clear.

Electabuzz and Mr. Mime are the front line heroes of "Psychic Buzz". Electabuzz represents the most cost efficient and longest lasting basic Pokémon in the game. Put him out in front in the beginning of the game to keep pressure on the opponent. Virtually no other monsters have a 2⸺ ⸺ attack that's capable of doing 40 ⸺ ⸺ punch combined with a para⸻⸺ ⸺ve and a huge 70 Hit Points ⸺ ⸺ arguably the best all around Basic Pokémon ⸺ the game.

Mr. Mime's attack move Meditate, plus its Invisible Wall Pokémon Power makes this Pokémon the most feared from the Jungle expansion. Meditate always starts off a little slow, but finishes huge. When used in combination with a Gengar using Curse from your bench, you can either speed up the demise of Mr. Mime's defender or stall it to take advantage of an good matchup. By transferring an additional damage counter onto the defender prior to your attack, Meditate might just have enough firepower to finish them off that turn. Or, by transferring a lone damage counter off the defender and onto a more feared benched Pokémon, Mr. Mime can strand a defender that's unable to sneak under his Invisible Wall.

Gengar is the top of the evolution line in a whole series of powerful Pokémon. Fossil Gastly has great Hit Points and a nice first turn attack move. No retreat cost and no weakness will guarantee that Fossil Gastly can tough it out for a few rounds of attack. Of course, this deck doesn't stop with Gastly for Psychic abilities. Evolve into Fossil Haunter as soon as possible. Haunter's Transparency Pokémon Power basically doubles the number of rounds that it can stay in battle without increasing Gastly's Hit Points. Again, no weakness and no retreat cost make Haunter useful for Nightmare attacking until a Gengar can be drawn. As soon as Gengar is drawn, retreat Haunter first, prior to evolving. You'll want to make the most use of Curse from your bench, and Gengar will require an energy discard in order to retreat.

PITFALLS: Just like the Pokémon that make this deck great, the major threats against it are fresh from the newly released Fossil expansion. Aerodactyl and Muk shut down "Psychic Buzz" by keeping all of its evolved Pokémon out of play, or turn off all the really cool Pokémon Powers that accompany them once they are in play. The best defense this deck has against these nasty opponents is Haunter's Nightmare attack move. Use a Gust of Wind to bring out the enemy Pokémon in question and disable it as soon as possible by putting it to sleep. On your next round, retreat Haunter (for free) and bring in a heavy hitter like Electabuzz to get the K-O and remove the threat for good.

WILDFIRE-DOT-DECK

Class: Stall Deck

Pokémon (12)
(4) Moltres
(4) Chansey
(4) Scyther

Energy (26)
(22) Fire Energy
(4) Double Colorless Energy

Trainers (22)
(3) Gambler
(2) Energy Retrieval
(2) Item Finder
(3) Scoop Up
(4) Energy Removal
(4) Super Energy Removal
(4) Pokémon Center

CONCEPTS: Here's a Stall deck with an obscure name. It's derived from Moltres' unique attack move along with the necessary filename extension that a certain online card game program adds: "Wildfire.dec". Stall is definitely the name of the game with Wildfire. Stall long enough to bring up a horrendously over-energized Moltres to K-O the opponent's deck in dying blow.

TIPS FOR PLAYING: As far as monsters in a stalling deck go, Chansey is the de-facto standard for slowing down an opponent's onslaught of attacks. With 120 Hit Points, it is the single biggest Basic Pokémon in the game. Scrunch is really the only attack move that should be utilized in this deck—The goal is to completely deprive your opponent of prize cards, and the self inflicted damage that Chansey's Double-edge attack entails is too detrimental. Only use Double-edge in extreme

situations where an opponent's K-O will seriously hurt their long term performance (if they have invested all of their energy onto the defending Pokémon or if their defending Pokémon is their only in-play monster for example.)

Scyther works remarkably well in stall decks because of its inherently large quantity of Hit Points for a basic Pokémon and the mobility that a free retreat provides. In addition, any Fighting type opponents will have a difficult time of breaking through Scyther's resistance. Preferably you can get multiple Scythers in play in order to totally abuse their free retreats, and fill your bench with multiple rounds of your opponent's attacks. Once your Scythers have had their fill it's time to bring in a few scrunching Chanseys, and eventually wipe the whole board clean with just one of your multiple Pokémon Center healing cards.

Moltres has a dual use in "Wildfire-dot-

Pokémon TCG Fossil Expansion Player's Guide

deck". The obvious function for this card is the Wildfire attack move. In fact, at least one of these legendary birds should be safe on your bench getting primed with Fire energy cards through most of the game. Wildfire is the ultimate "closer" for depleting your opponent's draw pile. However, additional copies of Moltres can be used for damage sponges when Chansey is hiding or when its Fighting resistance can be put to use. 70 Hit Points is not too shabby and should buy you a few rounds of time. Any Fire energy cards placed on Moltres are best used on a Wildfire attack, so avoid trying to retreat too often. Use Scoop Up as an effective means to get Moltres out of battle and cheat your opponent out of a Prize card they desperately are trying to earn.

Trainer cards included here to support the Stall theme include Gambler, Energy Removal, Super Energy Removal, and Pokémon Center. Gambler is genuinely risky to rely on when you really need new cards, but in a stall deck it takes on an all-new purpose—It can actually increase the size of your draw pile. Since every card in your hand is put back into your deck with Gambler, you shouldn't have to worry about depleting your deck faster than your opponent depletes their deck. If you do get "lucky" and draw 8 cards, you better make sure that your opponent has used at least 1 Professor Oak to keep your library the tallest.

Stall decks only work well when a significant number of the opponent's attack rounds can be voided through the Stall player's actions. After multiple turns of taking beatings, use up one of the four Pokémon Center cards in this deck to "start over". It is imperative that the solitary Moltres you are priming for a crushing Wildfire attack is completely damage free before using Pokémon Center! The Center requires the discard of all energy cards attached to monsters that it heals. However, if no damage counters exist on one of your Pokémon (and so Pokémon Center heals no damage to that monster) you are not required to discard any of its energy. If even a single damage counter is resident on the energy-laden Moltres, be sure to advance it for an early Wildfire. Make the most of this energy before the Pokémon Center tosses it.

Use Energy Removal and Super Energy Removal to discard key resources off of the most damaging of the other player's Pokémon. Try to select Double Colorless energy cards or specific color energy that the opponent's attacker is useless without. It will be impossible to totally deprive the opposition from enough energy to put on some kind of an offensive, so be prepared with scrunching Chanseys, retreating Scythers, and Scooped Up Moltres.

PITFALLS: Big-daddy, tournament-champion Haymaker should have plenty of trouble with Wildfire-dot-deck. Two thirds of the Pokémon in this deck are resistant to Fighting, and if absolutely necessary, Moltres' Dive Bomb attack can dispatch a pesky Scyther or two along the way. However, the other big deck archetype to fear—Rain Dance— will rip this deck apart. Wildfire-dot-deck is just too slow and too shallow to handle the beatings that a good mono-Water deck can inflict. In this situation it's best to hold your Energy Removal cards in your hand until you are certain the opponent has selected their prime attacker. Luckily for Wildfire, most Rain Dance decks make heavy use of Professor Oak to get what they need, so the number of rounds you will need to stall for should be drastically reduced. Hold fast and play smart!

KAMINARI

Class: Evolution Deck

Pokémon (22)
(4) Electabuzz
(4) Voltorb
(4) Base Set Electrode
(3) Fossil Zapdos
(4) Jungle Pikachu
(3) Fossil Raichu

Energy (21)
(21) Lightning Energy

Trainers (17)
(3) Bill
(2) Professor Oak
(3) Pokémon Trader
(3) Energy Retrieval
(1) Item Finder
(3) Switch
(2) Scoop Up

CONCEPTS: "Kaminari" is the Romaji word for the "Lightning" class of Pokémon Types. This "Kaminari" deck is dedicated to all the themes that make Lightning such a destructive force: Defender destruction, bench destruction, and plenty of self destruction. This can barely be classified an "Evolution" deck when both evolutions are only Stage 1. And the Electrodes are only really included for their Buzzap Pokémon Power and getting some Fossil Zapdos powered up for attacking.

TIPS FOR PLAYING: Your entire focus when playing Kaminari is to beat away at your opponent's bench while trying to keep your own bench safe from self inflicted damage. Bench Destruction has been a theme in existence since the original Base set of Pokémon TCG cards were released, but only now after the Fossil expansion came out do we have a truly viable tournament ready Bench Destruction deck.

Jungle Pikachu, Fossil Raichu, and Fossil Zapdos are the Pokémon best fitting the theme of Kaminari. Pikachu and Raichu are the most selective of these Pokémon, allowing you to choose

the benched monsters that you attack. Always choose the Pokémon that your opponent is developing for future rounds of attack. Typically this will be the Pokémon with an evolution or two in place and lots of energy cards. Zapdos absolutely loves a full bench to Thunderstorm! There is plenty of coin flipping fun to be had here.

Use Electabuzz early in the game when energy is at a minimum and you want to apply the most pressure possible. Don't be afraid to Switch him out or even Scoop him up when his time has come. That's what these trainer cards are included for.

PITFALLS: This deck is very weak to Fighting type opponents. Fortunately Zapdos' resistance will come in handy during these match-ups. Be certain that every Pokémon on your bench is ready to attack, so an untimely Gust of Wind or Energy Removal by the opposing player doesn't put you into a bad situation. Always be prepared for these kind of disruptive trainers by keeping only powered up Pokémon on your bench, preferably with multiple options to choose from.

Pokémon TCG Fossil Expansion Player's Guide

MONSTER SWAP

Class: Stall Deck

Pokémon (20)
(4) Onix
(3) Mankey
(4) Mr. Mime
(3) Doduo
(3) Dodrio
(3) Chansey

Energy (22)
(9) Fighting Energy
(9) Psychic Energy
(4) Double Colorless Energy

Trainers (18)
(2) Gambler
(4) Poke Ball
(3) Maintenance
(3) Defender
(2) Gust of Wind
(2) Lass
(2) Impostor Professor Oak

CONCEPTS: Here's a deck designed to make use of two complementary Pokémon abilities. Mr. Mime's Invisible Wall Pokémon Power is almost entirely the opposite of Onix's Harden attack move. Mr. Mime can block the defenders with big damage attacks, and Onix can block all those opponents with the small attacks. Rather than play a guessing game about what the opponent may be playing, use both of these Pokémon to be prepared for any situation.

TIPS FOR PLAYING: Gamblers and Poke Balls are used to set the combo up without sacrificing deck size too much. Neither is entirely reliable so be prepared if the coin doesn't flip exactly like you'd like it. All three main Pokémon components are necessary to properly defend against most opponents, so don't stop manipulating your deck until Mr. Mime, Onix, and Dodrio are all in place.

Once all these monsters are in play, just swap them back and forth as necessary to defend against the opponent and stall your way to the winner's circle. Dodrio is a key to winning with this deck. Multiple Dodrios will pro-

vide additive Retreat Aid benefits, and are a good idea with Onix's high retreat cost. Dodrio really allows the "Swap" in "Monster Swap" to shine through.

Mankey and Lass have been added so that you can sneak Peeks at the opponent's hand. With more than one Mankey in play you should get an eyeful every turn! Lass not only will discard the opponent's Trainer cards, but allows you to see what they have left since they must show you their hand when Lass is played. When the time feels right (and using Mankey to constantly Peek at their top Library card will help you know this), use Impostor Professor Oak to toss their hand back into their deck.

PITFALLS: There is a surprising balance to the Pokémon in this deck. Rarely will a weakness issue be your downfall. However, you do need to be wary of running yourself out of cards before your opponent. Maintenance has been included in place of the card drawing ability of Bill. You draw fewer cards than Bill, but restocking you draw pile with extra cards from your hand is welcome in this stall deck.

FEROCIOUS COMMONS

Class: Beat-Down Deck

Pokémon (16)
(4) Rattata
(4) Raticate
(4) Staryu
(4) Machop

Energy (16)
(8) Fighting Energy
(8) Water Energy

Trainers (28)
(4) Professor Oak
(4) Bill
(4) Energy Search
(4) PlusPower
(4) Gust of Wind
(4) Energy Removal
(4) Super Energy Removal

CONCEPTS: It's lean. It's mean. And it's cheap! All the best first turn attacking common cards in the game have been thrown together in maximum quantities to make up "Ferocious Commons". Combined with all the disruptive trainer cards necessary to hurt the opponent as much, and as fast as possible, this deck should earn plenty of respect for its Pokémon trainer. And due to its simplicity in construction and strategy, it can be great fun for beginning players to start with.

TIPS FOR PLAYING: Rattata, Staryu, and Machop are all willing and able to attack for 20 damage on the first turn. There is no other deck where the "who goes first" coin flip is so important! These little monsters need to be taking the lead in the race to deal damage. Only Rattata will see minor support from an evolution card as the game progresses. However, do not expend additional resources on Raticate as

Hyper Fang is so frequently less useful than the energy cards that it takes to power it. Just keep plugging away with 20 base damage per round from each of these monsters. Don't slow up. Each of your attackers should stay in battle to the bitter end!

Of course, retreating to avoid a bad match-up in weakness for yourself, or preferably making the most of a bad match-up for your opponent is perfectly acceptable here. "Ferocious Commons" is extremely low in its energy consumption, so a minor discard here and there for retreat purposes is acceptable. But only when the retreating Pokémon is replaced with another fighting machine ready to attack. Every single round needs to end with you dealing at least 20 damage.

This deck was designed to wield the fastest possible attacking deck with the fewest number of expensive cards. The only four rare cards in this deck are all Super Energy Removals and these could be easily replaced with something less valuable. Recycle would easily fit the theme here with its ability to put those Energy Removals or PlusPowers back on top of your draw pile for quick reuse.

Professor Oak, Bill, and Energy Search all give you card advantage. Card advantage is a very simple concept: If you have more cards than your opponent can deal with, you will have the upper hand. Bill is never a bad draw. Using 4 Bill cards increases your normal one-card draw for that turn into two cards, and giving you more options in your hand to work with. Also, 4 Bill in a deck effectively reduces the deck size to 56 cards, and increasing the probability that every random draw will be a good one. Energy Search is included here for all these same reasons. Every copy reduces your "random" deck size as well as yielding the exact energy card needed in any situation. And of course Professor Oak provides card advantage like no other card can. It is potentially the most powerful card in the game. In this "Ferocious Commons" deck, Professor Oak should always be used as soon as you have depleted all options in your hand. Don't worry about which few cards you may be saving for some future event. Use Professor Oak—better cards are sure to come!

PlusPower and Gust of Wind are included as "surprise" cards. Try to catch the opponent off-guard when you use them. PlusPower is remarkably useful during the early rounds of a match. Its great to see another player's face when four PlusPower on a Rattata dishes out as much as 60 damage on the first turn. And if this 60 damage is best dumped onto one of your opponent's benched monsters, use the mighty Gust of Wind to invite them to the party first!

PITFALLS: Be careful to use your trainer cards wisely and choose targets that have the potential to create the most problems for this deck. There is no depth to "Ferocious Commons". Typically, if you can't force an opponent completely out of Pokémon in-play and finish the game early, you will see your Pokémon faint faster than you can draw new ones out of your deck. Again, Professor Oak will be key to your strategy. If you hesitate to toss your existing hand when victory is potentially only one attack away, the opportunity may very well be lost for good.

Damage Swap decks are the death of "Ferocious Commons". Luckily, most of those decks are pretty darn slow, and they will rarely be able to get an Alakazam or even a Slowbro into play to whisk away your attacks. If your opponent does manage to get one of these monsters out, use a quick Gust of Wind to bring them forward and introduce them to the business end of a Raticate!

CURSED SWAP

Class: Evolution Deck

Pokémon (24)
(4) Fossil Gastly
(3) Fossil Haunter
(2) Gengar
(4) Abra
(3) Kadabra
(2) Alakazam
(2) Mr. Mime
(4) Chansey

Energy (20)
(20) Psychic Energy

Trainers (16)
(3) Professor Oak
(3) Computer Search
(3) Pokémon Trader
(3) Pokémon Center
(2) Mr. Fuji
(2) Energy Retrieval

CONCEPTS: The "Curse of the Gengar" adds a whole new dimension to traditional Alakazam decks. This deck (affectionately titled "Cursed Swap") is significantly more true to the roots of Damage Swap decks than the "Psychic Buzz" deck shown earlier. Here we aren't sacrificing the stalling aspects necessary to ensure Alakazam's safe arrival like the Lightning/Psychic deck does, and stalling to victory is not necessarily out of the question. There are a lot of options in this deck to make use of, and a versatile Pokémon trainer will never be at a loss for a winning strategy.

TIPS FOR PLAYING: Against another Stall deck you "Cursed Swap" should definitely be going for the K-O. There is too many necessary card drawing trainers in here. Besides, Gengar will scare your stalling opponent into using their Pokémon Centers early. And if they are foolish enough to leave a benched Pokémon only 10 damage away from fainting, make use of Gengar's Curse to finish the job. There are plenty of weapons here to get that damage flowing. Kadabra, Gengar, Mr. Mime and even Chansey are all offenses to fear. Keep a Haunter available to force opponents asleep with his Nightmare attack move. With a few lucky coin flips (unlucky for your opponent) the opposing Pokémon will be sleeping like a baby instead of concentrating on stalling like it should.

Against an evolution machine like Rain Dance or a Vileplume deck, definitely look to stall your opponent out. The key will be to get Alakazam in play along with several Chanseys for damage soaking. Mr. Fuji is included to heal a single benched damage sponge, and fill your deck with cards to keep you safely behind your opponent in the race to the end of your decks. Pokémon Center was made for this kind of deck—in a single turn eliminate many rounds of damage that your opponent worked so hard to inflict.

Pokémon TCG Fossil Expansion Player's Guide

Against a beat-down deck like Haymaker, "Cursed Swap" can go either way. Both Stall and Psychic offense are at your disposal in this situation. Let the opponent's deck provide the cues necessary to "Cursed Swap" correctly. Keep your eye on their weaknesses and their speed. A quick flurry of activity by a Haymaker player will mean they are sacrificing the long game to apply pressure. Use Pokémon Traders and Professor Oak to get your Damage Swap lock in place so you can sit this one out. However, if the Haymaker opponent is slower to jump into their deck and is sporting lots of fashionable Fighting Pokémon (which are usually weak to Psychic), don't be afraid to beat them at their own game. Nothing frightens away a Hitmonchan like a fully powered Kadabra!

In a stall situation, if your Scrunching Chansey is failing a fair share of coin flips and taking on damage, just retreat it out. Likewise, if Chansey applied pressure with a Double-edge attack you'll want to get it back to your bench ASAP. Once benched then play Mr. Fuji on it. It will return to your deck along with the energy cards attached to it, which should give you some additional insurance against decking yourself. The added energy returned to your deck will be appreciated later in the game as well, as this deck has to sacrifice several energy slots to make room for more Pokémon and Trainer cards. As if these were not reasons enough for you to revel in the beauty of Mr. Fuji, keeping your opponent from drawing a prize card is the pinnacle of its usefulness.

Professor Oak is included in "Cursed Swap" as the major card advantage component of the deck. Typically Gambler with its ability to let you put an entire hand of unneeded Pokémon or energy cards back into your deck is more appropriate for a Stall deck. However, the uncertainty that Gambler brings with it is the key reason that this deck will stay away from using it. An easy variant to experiment with here would include a few copies of each Professor Oak and Gambler. After some play testing it should be a relatively easy task to decide which card drawing machine fits your playing style the best.

PITFALLS: Muk is the single biggest threat to a deck like this. Without the use of Pokémon Powers, Alakazam is a lame duck Pokémon with no hope for lasting in battle more than a few rounds. In this situation, stick to Kadabra for offensive damage and Haunter for status effects. With mindful use of Pokémon Centers and retreating Chanseys there may be hope for pulling out a stall victory.

Also, there is a severe lack of energy cards in this deck. A few Energy Retrieval trainer cards have been included to combat this, but against an opponent packing four of each Energy Removal and Super Energy Removal will be very difficult to create an offense against. Revert to your stall tactics and use Fossil Gastly's Energy Conversion attack move in a worst case situation. Be mindful of your energy drops, selecting only those monsters that you have in play that really need them to obtain your goal.

U.S. COLLECTOR'S GUIDE

U.S. game company Wizards of the Coast (WOTC) is responsible for bringing the Pokémon Trading Card Game to North America. It's a licensed adaptation from the Japanese Pocket Monsters Card Game first released in 1996. For a company as experienced and innovative in the card game arena as Wizards, merely translating an existing game to create the Pokémon TCG was a pretty tame task. However, even though individual card functionality remains unchanged from the Japanese game, the product bundling and marketing is somewhat different. Americans can expect to see all the same cards that the core Japanese game entails, but will need to buy different types of packaging to get those cards.

102 CARD BASE SET

STARTER DECKS

Wizards of the Coast first released its Pokémon TCG "Starter Decks" after Thanksgiving in November 1998. A Starter deck contains everything that 2 players will need to begin playing the Trading Card Game. There are two different 30-card decks included along with rulebooks, damage counters, a holographic "Chansey" coin, and a limited print holographic "Machamp" card as a bonus. All cards in the Starter Deck are unlimited print run versions (they do not contain the "Edition 1" stamp),

2-Player Starter Set

except for the premium Machamp card which does contain the limited print run stamp.

The "Starter" rulebook is a small fold-out sheet that describes a very basic method of learning and playing the TCG. Both 30-card decks included have been optimized for this entry-level set of rules. One of the two decks is comprised entirely of Fighting Pokémon, Fighting Energy cards, and Trainer cards. The other deck is all Fire type cards. When played against one another, these two decks give an excellent overview of the base game play mechanics necessary to run a typical Pokémon match. They are reasonably balanced so that neither "starting" player will dominate matches, and they give a very good impression for some of the themes that the different color types maintain—Fire is powerful but expensive, while Fighting is strong but without depth.

30-CARD FIGHTING STARTER DECK	30-CARD FIRE STARTER DECK
Pokémon (12)	**Pokémon (11)**
(3) Diglett	(4) Ponyta
(4) Machop	(4) Charmander
(2) Machoke	(2) Charmeleon
(2) Rattata	(1) Growlithe
(1) Dratini	**Trainers (5)**
Trainers (4)	(1) Bill
(2) Potion	(1) Gust of Wind
(1) Energy Removal	(2) Switch
(1) Pokédex	(1) Energy Retrieval
Energy (14)	**Energy (14)**
(14) Fighting Energy	(14) Fire Energy

Even though the Starter rules are simplistic, they are (for the most part) legitimate references for official "advanced" level games.

Everything in the Starter rule sheet is an accurate introduction to the full set of rules. They are just toned down a bit to make the learning process easier. None of the most confusing aspects of the full-blown version of the game are presented when these two starter decks battle one another. For example, Weakness and Resistance is never discussed and would never need to be calculated with these two decks. Also, most of these Pokémon have very straightforward attack moves with no lingering "effects" to keep track of. All new players to the Pokémon Trading Card Game will want to get plenty of practice time in on one of these Starter Deck packages (before moving on to the more advanced Theme Decks available).

BASE SET BOOSTER PACKS

The Base set booster packs were the next major product release for the Pokémon TCG. During late January of 1999 many large retail chains (like Target and Wal-Mart) were receiving the first big shipments of these packs. Base set Booster packs contain 11 cards with a random assortment of cards in all rarities. There is always 1 rare card, 3 uncommon cards, 5 common cards, and 2 basic energy cards (which do not have rarity symbols). On average, only 1 pack out of every 3 will contain a premium (holographic) rare card with the other 2 packs containing non-holographic rare cards.

There are 2 different "Editions" for each booster set including the Base set:

- **LIMITED** print run cards (commonly referred to as "1st Edition" cards): These cards contain a special "Edition 1" stamp on the face identifying it as a card from the first print run of production. The stamp is located in different spots depending upon whether it is a Pokémon, Energy or Trainer card, but the stamp is always easy to

"Edition 1" stamped cards are more valuable.

identify. Limited print cards were made once and will not be printed again. Their quantity is fixed and pre-determined by WOTC. These cards represent the most collectible of all booster pack offerings in the market since their availability is strictly rationed.

- **UNLIMITED** print run cards (many times incorrectly referred to as "2nd Edition" cards): These cards are identical in every respect to "Limited" print cards, except that they do not contain the "Edition 1" stamp. These cards do not have a fixed print run size, and WOTC will continue to print these cards until they decide to discontinue the product line. There is no guarantee how many (or how few) of these version cards will eventually reach retail stores

The very first shipments of booster packs to reach the retail market contained the limited print "Edition 1" stamp. Unlimited print run cards (without this stamp) were not present in retail until late February.

The Base Set is made up of 102 unique cards, but only 101 of these can be found in Booster packs. The Machamp card (# 8/102) can only be obtained from Starter Decks. This should give players an added incentive to begin their collections with the Starter Deck—which does the best job at teaching the rules of the game. Despite what many collectors think however, the remaining 15 holographic cards in the set are evenly distributed in the boosters at a 1 in 3 pack ratio. There

The Machamp card can only be found in the Starter Set (see opposite page).

are just as many Charizards printed and distributed as every other holographic in the set (like Magneton or Raichu). Due to the popularity of certain premium cards (like Charizard, Blastoise and Alakazam) however, their availability and secondary market value will be significantly different than other (less popular) cards with the same rarity.

Many cards made it to print with minor errors in their text, artwork, or layout. These types of misprints are typically corrected for future print runs as soon as they are identified. When this happens, slightly different revisions of cards end up in the card singles market simultaneously. In fact, the cards in the Base set have displayed the most changes over time:

- Picture Shadow and 99 in Copyright cards - One of the most noticeable changes to the Base set occurred in mid-March of 1999. All cards printed prior to this point had "99" included in Nintendo's copyright information on the bottom of each card. This was apparently an error and was removed in all subsequent printings. Also, the "shadow" that borders the picture on newer TCG cards was missing from the oldest of Base set print runs. Along with removing "99" and adding a shadow, at this same time many subtle changes to colors and fonts also occurred—colors seem to get darker and the fonts less defined.
- Length, Length and cards - Early revisions of Bulbasaur and Kakuna cards incorrectly identified the Pokémon's Weight as "Length". The text directly underneath the artwork was subsequently corrected but many of these "Length, Length" cards are still around.
- Reversed HP cards - U.S. Pokémon TCG cards show a Pokémon's Hit Points in the top right corner of the card (50 HP for example). In Japan, the original Pocket Monster card design gives the number last (as in HP 50). This "Japanese style" HP description was misprinted onto many early copies of Base set's Caterpie, Metapod, and Vulpix cards.
- Monster Ball Voltorbs - The "flavor" text at the very bottom of early copies of the Voltorb card referred to this Pokémon as a "Monster Ball". It was later corrected to accurately describe it as a "Poke Ball".
- Red-Cheek Pikachu - Pikachu is normally shown with red cheeks. The Jungle Pikachu card shows the electric mouse with red cheeks. However, the Base set version of this card is apparently supposed to have yellow cheeks. This seems to be a confusing matter for Wizards. Even though very early copies of the Base set Pikachu contained the (correct) yellow cheeks, subsequent copies of the card showed (incorrect) red cheeks. The mis-corrected correction was eventually corrected however! (whoa... that's a mouthful!) All Base set Pikachu cards are printed with yellow cheeks once again.
- Sideways Fist Diglett - This misprint didn't enter the mix until very late in the printing cycle, and appears to be limited to only a fraction of all Diglett cards in production. Next to Diglett's "Dig" attack move is a single "Fist" (Fighting Energy symbol). Some Digletts apparently have the "Fist" pointing to the side, rather than straight up and down as it should be.
- No Damage Ninetales - On very few copies of the Ninetales holographic card (most of them reportedly from "Brushfire" Theme decks) the attack damage ("80") next to its Fire Blast attack move is missing. Now that is one heck of a lame attack! Four Fire energy required, and discard a Fire energy in order to do zero damage!

BASE SET THEME DECKS

Four pre-constructed "Theme Decks" were released during late January 1999. Instead of the "Beginner" level rules designation that the Starter decks received, all of the subsequent pre-constructed Theme decks are designated as "Advanced" level. Each different type of theme deck contains 60 cards, designed to work as a ready-to-play, official Pokémon TCG deck. Each Theme deck contains monster cards from 2 different game "colors", and when combined, all four Base set theme decks cover the spectrum of the 6 different colors available.

Each of the Theme decks includes one premium holographic card. It is a different premium card for each version of Theme deck, but it is a guaranteed method of obtaining an unlimited print copy of these holographic

cards. For example, the Overgrowth Theme deck always contains a Gyarados holographic card. In addition to the 60-card deck, each Theme deck contains a holographic collectible coin, damage counters, and the same advanced level (larger) rulebook that accompanies the Starter decks. Since these Theme decks were not designed to be split into two separate 30-card decks, the smaller Starter rules sheet is not included here.

64 CARD JUNGLE EXPANSION

JUNGLE EXPANSION BOOSTER PACKS
Trading card games are continuously refreshed with new sets of cards released on a periodic basis. These new sets are referred to as "Expansion" sets. In June 1999 the first expansion set for the Pokémon TCG was officially released. "Jungle" hit store shelves and set new records for opening day sales at many retail locations. Jungle expansion Booster packs contain 11 cards just like the Base set, but the rarity distribution and makeup was slightly different. Instead of 5 common cards and 2 basic energy cards, the Jungle boosters do not contain energy cards. The booster pack make-up became 1 rare card, 3 uncommon cards, and 7 common cards. Also, just like the Base set, an average of only 1 pack out of 3 will contain a premium (holographic) rare card with the other 2

packs containing non-holographic rare cards.

Other than the set list number at the bottom, Jungle expansion cards can be easily recognized by a small tropical flower symbol printed on their face. Monster cards have this symbol outside

Jungle cards are marked with a leaf emblem.

the lower right corner of the artwork, and the solitary Trainer card from the set (Poke Ball) shows this symbol at the bottom of the text instruction box. In addition to the expansion symbol, a limited print run of Jungle cards also received the coveted "Edition 1" stamp. "Edition 1" cards required less than 2 weeks to sell out at most retail locations.

One of the most noteworthy product configuration changes that Wizards of the Coast implemented was an increase in the set size of Jungle

from the Japanese release. Japanese Jungle contained a grand total of 48 new cards. This breaks down into 16 rares, 16 uncommons, and 16 commons. Although Wizards accurately translated and recreated all of these cards from Japanese Jungle, they duplicated the 16 most rare cards as both premium "holographic", and non-holographic versions. This bumped the total U.S. set size up to 64 cards, but maintains only 48 functionally unique cards for players to utilize in decks.

In Japan, every single Jungle booster pack contains a holographic rare card. They must contain one—there are no non-holographic copies of the rare cards to distribute in packs. However, Wizards "remedied" this oversight and gave Pokémon collectors 16 additional cards to pursue. And by maintaining the ultra-rare (1 in 3 booster) holographic frequency that is present in the Base set, these additional 16 cards are accompanied by a fairly hefty price tag.

As was the case in the Base set, a few minor (and one pretty major) misprints surfaced on Jungle expansion cards:

• Wrong Art Electrode - All "Edition 1" copies of the non-holographic Electrode card from the Jungle expansion were printed with the wrong artwork in place. Instead of the new art that's seen in holographic

The first "Edition 1" Electrode cards feature the wrong artwork, which was lifted from the original Electrode cards. This makes them even more collectible.

copies of Jungle Electrode, the non-holographic versions use Electrode's artwork from the Base set. The misprint card can

still clearly be identified as a "Jungle expansion" card by its attack moves, set number, and the tropical flower Jungle expansion symbol printed on the face of the card.

• Edition "d" Butterfree - On about half of all limited print Butterfree cards, the "1" in the "Edition 1" stamp looks very much like a lowercase "d". Since limited print cards are never reprinted, this error was not corrected, but multiple copies of both "1" and "d" cards exist.

• Evolution Errors - Early revisions of both Rapidash and Seaking have incorrect text identifying their predecessor evolution stages. In the upper right corner of the card, instead of stating: "Put Rapidash/Seaking on the Basic Pokémon" (as it should say), it incorrectly states: "Put Rapidash/Seaking on the Stage 1 card". This is a very minor misprint, but notable.

JUNGLE EXPANSION THEME DECKS

Two pre-constructed Jungle Theme Decks were first released at the same time limited print Jungle boosters were available. Like the Base set decks, these Theme decks are designated as "Advanced" level rules. Each of the decks include one premium holographic card. But unlike the Base set Theme decks, these Jungle expansion decks do not also contain another rare card. Check the U.S. set lists (coming up) for a better description of these decks and their contents.

Pokémon TCG Fossil Expansion Player's Guide

62 CARD FOSSIL EXPANSION

FOSSIL EXPANSION BOOSTER PACKS

In late September 1999 the second expansion set for the Pokémon TCG was released. "Fossil" was shipping to retailers at the same time that Wizards of the Coast's online store was shipping directly to consumers. This card set marked the first time that unlimited print run cards were hitting the market simultaneously to limited "Edition 1" cards. In many locations, unlimited boosters arrived *before* limited, which frustrated hardcore collectors looking for only the most valuable of packs.

Fossil expansion Booster packs contain 11 cards with the exact same rarity distribution and makeup as Jungle expansion packs. This is 1 rare (1 in 3 chance of it being a premium "holographic" card), 3 uncommons, and 7 common cards. Card numbers at the bottom of Fossil cards will all have a set size of "62". This number, along with the Fossil expansion symbol (a small skeleton hand) that's printed on the face of each card helps identify Fossil expansion cards from the previous 2 sets.

Fossil cards are marked with a skeletal foot emblem.

Mew is one of the most popular Pokémon, and was in the Japanese Fossil set, but not the US set.

Based on Japanese Fossil, the anticipated U.S. expansion was expected to be 64 cards in total size. Japanese Fossil is 48 cards with only holographic copies of the 16 rare cards. Knowing what happened with Jungle, WOTC would most likely duplicate those 16 cards as non-holographic for a grand total of 64 cards in the North American set. This is not what happened however. Wizards left out a key rare card from the Fossil expansion bringing the set size down to 62. Pokémon #151 "Mew" is revered by many Pokémon Trainers as the most rare and elusive of all Pocket Monsters. Unfortunately Mew, which was included in the Japanese version of Fossil, is only available as a special promotional card in the U.S. Although not an overly powerful card, Wizards considered this Pokémon "unique" and decided not to include it in booster packs.

Wizards of the Coast has progressively gotten better at catching errors in card layouts before printing the first run. The U.S. Fossil expansion contains only 1 major misprint:

- Holographic Zapdos - The earliest copies of this holographic card have foil inlay that is "missing" the upper left-hand corner. Careful inspection of the missing foil should reveal it to match the inlays for holographic Evolution Pokémon cards. The upper left-hand corner is typically where a picture of the pre-evolved stage of a Pokémon is placed. Zapdos must have originally been slated as an evolved Pokémon (which it is not) and the wrong foil inlay was used.

FOSSIL EXPANSION THEME DECKS

Just like Jungle, two new Fossil pre-constructed Theme Decks were released when the set was first released. These two Theme decks ("Bodyguard" and "Lock Down") come complete with one premium holographic card as part of a 60 card deck, and an all-new holographic (Aerodactyl) collectible coin. These coins are still a far cry from the quality of the plastic foil coins that accompany Japanese

Theme decks, but the U.S. Fossil coins are definitely the nicest ones produced by Wizards of the Coast. Check the U.S. set lists (rest of this chapter) for a better description of these decks and their contents.

"BASIC SET" or "STARTER SET" (SERIES 1)

U.S. SET COMPOSITION

The "Base Set" is the first Pokémon Trading Card Game set released by Wizards of the Coast in the U.S. The limited print Base set was released in January 1999. The unlimited print run cards began selling in February 1999.

102 TOTAL CARDS

AVAILABLE IN:
"STARTER" DECKS:
• $8.99 U.S.
• Holographic "Chansey" paper coin
• 10 damage counters
• "Starter" Level Rules Sheet
• "Advanced" Level Rulebook
• 61 cards (capable of being split into two 30-card "starter" decks with special rules for learning to play the game)
• Fixed set of cards (every Starter Deck comes with the following cards):

BY RARITY

16	Ultra-Rare Holographic
16	Rare (non-Holographic)
32	Uncommon
32	Common
6	Basic Energy (no rarity)

Pokémon (23)
(3) Diglett
(4) Machop
(2) Machoke
(1) Machamp
(4) Ponyta
(4) Charmander
(2) Charmeleon
(1) Growlithe
(2) Rattata
(1) Dratini

Trainer Cards (9)
(2) Potion
(1) Energy Removal
(1) Pokédex
(1) Energy Retrieval
(1) Bill
(1) Gust of Wind
(2) Switch

Energy (28)
(14) Fighting Energy
(14) Fire Energy

2-Player Starter Set

AVAILABLE IN:

"BOOSTER" PACKS:

- $3.29 U.S.
- 11 cards (randomly packaged):
  - 1 Rare / Ultra-Rare cards
  - 3 Uncommon cards
  - 5 Common cards
  - 2 Basic Energy cards (no rarity)
- When purchased through booster packs, card rarities are distributed as:
  - 1:33 = 3% Ultra-Rare (holographic) cards
  - 2:33 = 6% Rare (non-holographic) cards
  - 9:33 = 27% Uncommon cards
  - 15:33 = 45% Common cards
  - 6:33 = 18% Basic Energy cards

"THEME" DECKS:

- $8.99 U.S.
- Holographic "Chansey" paper coin
- 10 damage counters
- "Advanced" Level Rulebook
- 60 cards
- Fixed set of cards (every Theme Deck comes with the following cards):

ZAP!

Pokémon (21)

- (1) Mewtwo
- (3) Abra
- (1) Kadabra
- (3) Gastly
- (2) Haunter
- (2) Jynx
- (2) Drowzee
- (4) Pikachu
- (3) Magnemite

Trainer Cards (11)

- (2) Bill
- (1) Professor Oak
- (1) Computer Search
- (2) Gust of Wind
- (2) Switch
- (1) Defender
- (1) Potion
- (1) Super Potion

Energy (28)

- (16) Psychic Energy
- (12) Lightning Energy

OVERGROWTH

Pokémon (23)

- (4) Weedle
- (2) Kakuna
- (1) Beedrill
- (4) Bulbasaur
- (2) Ivysaur
- (4) Staryu
- (3) Starmie
- (2) Magikarp
- (1) Gyarados

Trainer Cards (9)

- (2) Bill
- (2) Gust of Wind
- (2) Switch
- (1) Potion
- (2) Super Potion

Energy (28)

- (16) Grass Energy
- (12) Water Energy

BRUSHFIRE

Pokémon (22)

- (4) Charmander
- (2) Charmeleon
- (2) Growlithe
- (1) Arcanine
- (2) Vulpix
- (1) Ninetales
- (4) Nidoran (M)
- (4) Weedle
- (2) Tangela

Trainer Cards (10)

- (1) PlusPower
- (1) Gust of Wind
- (1) Energy Removal
- (1) Switch
- (3) Potion
- (2) Energy Retrieval
- (1) Lass

Energy (28)

- (18) Fire Energy
- (10) Grass Energy

BLACKOUT

Pokémon (24)

- (1) Hitmonchan
- (4) Machop
- (2) Machoke
- (3) Sandshrew
- (3) Onix
- (3) Staryu
- (4) Squirtle
- (2) Wartortle
- (2) Farfetch'd

Trainer Cards (8)

- (1) Professor Oak
- (1) PlusPower
- (1) Gust of Wind
- (4) Energy Removal
- (1) Super Energy Removal

Energy (28)

- (16) Fighting Energy
- (12) Water Energy

102-CARD "BASE" SET

1st Edition released January 1999
Unlimited print run released February 1999

CARD	RARITY	COLOR	LEVEL	NUM	NAME
1/102	Holographic	Psychic	lv 42	#065	Alakazam
2/102	Holographic	Water	lv 52	#009	Blastoise
3/102	Holographic	Colorless	lv 55	#113	Chansey
4/102	Holographic	Fire	lv 76	#006	Charizard
5/102	Holographic	Colorless	lv 14	#035	Clefairy
6/102	Holographic	Water	lv 41	#130	Gyarados
7/102	Holographic	Fighting	lv 33	#107	Hitmonchan
8/102	Holographic	Fighting	lv 67	#068	Machamp
9/102	Holographic	Lightning	lv 28	#082	Magneton
10/102	Holographic	Psychic	lv 53	#150	Mewtwo
11/102	Holographic	Grass	lv 48	#034	Nidoking
12/102	Holographic	Fire	lv 32	#038	Ninetales
13/102	Holographic	Water	lv 48	#062	Poliwrath
14/102	Holographic	Lightning	lv 40	#026	Raichu
15/102	Holographic	Grass	lv 67	#003	Venusaur
16/102	Holographic	Lightning	lv 64	#145	Zapdos
17/102	Rare	Grass	lv 32	#015	Beedrill
18/102	Rare	Colorless	lv 33	#148	Dragonair
19/102	Rare	Fighting	lv 36	#051	Dugtrio
20/102	Rare	Lightning	lv 35	#125	Electabuzz
21/102	Rare	Lightning	lv 40	#101	Electrode
22/102	Rare	Colorless	lv 36	#017	Pidgeotto
23/102	Uncommon	Fire	lv 45	#059	Arcanine
24/102	Uncommon	Fire	lv 32	#005	Charmeleon
25/102	Uncommon	Water	lv 42	#087	Dewgong
26/102	Uncommon	Colorless	lv 10	#147	Dratini
27/102	Uncommon	Colorless	lv 20	#083	Farfetch'd
28/102	Uncommon	Fire	lv 18	#058	Growlithe
29/102	Uncommon	Psychic	lv 22	#093	Haunter
30/102	Uncommon	Grass	lv 20	#002	Ivysaur
31/102	Uncommon	Psychic	lv 23	#124	Jynx
32/102	Uncommon	Psychic	lv 38	#064	Kadabra
33/102	Uncommon	Grass	lv 23	#014	Kakuna
34/102	Uncommon	Fighting	lv 40	#067	Machoke
35/102	Uncommon	Water	lv 08	#129	Magikarp
36/102	Uncommon	Fire	lv 24	#126	Magmar
37/102	Uncommon	Grass	lv 25	#033	Nidorino
38/102	Uncommon	Water	lv 28	#061	Poliwhirl
39/102	Uncommon	Colorless	lv 12	#137	Porygon
40/102	Uncommon	Colorless	lv 41	#020	Raticate
41/102	Uncommon	Water	lv 12	#086	Seel
42/102	Uncommon	Water	lv 22	#008	Wartortle
43/102	Common	Psychic	lv 10	#063	Abra
44/102	Common	Grass	lv 13	#001	Bulbasaur
45/102	Common	Grass	lv 13	#010	Caterpie
46/102	Common	Fire	lv 10	#004	Charmander
47/102	Common	Fighting	lv 08	#050	Diglett
48/102	Common	Colorless	lv 10	#084	Doduo

CARD	RARITY	COLOR	LEVEL	NUM	NAME
49/102	Common	Psychic	lv 12	#096	Drowzee
50/102	Common	Psychic	lv 08	#092	Gastly
51/102	Common	Grass	lv 13	#109	Koffing
52/102	Common	Fighting	lv 20	#066	Machop
53/102	Common	Lightning	lv 13	#081	Magnemite
54/102	Common	Grass	lv 21	#011	Metapod
55/102	Common	Grass	lv 20	#032	Nidoran (M)
56/102	Common	Fighting	lv 12	#095	Onix
57/102	Common	Colorless	lv 08	#016	Pidgey
58/102	Common	Lightning	lv 12	#025	Pikachu
59/102	Common	Water	lv 13	#060	Poliwag
60/102	Common	Fire	lv 10	#077	Ponyta
61/102	Common	Colorless	lv 09	#019	Rattata
62/102	Common	Fighting	lv 12	#027	Sandshrew
63/102	Common	Water	lv 08	#007	Squirtle
64/102	Common	Water	lv 28	#121	Starmie
65/102	Common	Water	lv 15	#120	Staryu
66/102	Common	Grass	lv 08	#114	Tangela
67/102	Common	Lightning	lv 10	#100	Voltorb
68/102	Common	Fire	lv 11	#037	Vulpix
69/102	Common	Grass	lv 12	#013	Weedle
70/102	Rare	Trainer			Clefairy Doll
71/102	Rare	Trainer			Computer Search
72/102	Rare	Trainer			Devolution Spray
73/102	Rare	Trainer			Impostor Professor Oak
74/102	Rare	Trainer			Item Finder
75/102	Rare	Trainer			Lass
76/102	Rare	Trainer			Pokémon Breeder
77/102	Rare	Trainer			Pokémon Trader
78/102	Rare	Trainer			Scoop Up
79/102	Rare	Trainer			Super Energy Removal
80/102	Uncommon	Trainer			Defender
81/102	Uncommon	Trainer			Energy Retrieval
82/102	Uncommon	Trainer			Full Heal
83/102	Uncommon	Trainer			Maintenance
84/102	Uncommon	Trainer			PlusPower
85/102	Uncommon	Trainer			Pokémon Center
86/102	Uncommon	Trainer			Pokémon Flute
87/102	Uncommon	Trainer			Pokédex
88/102	Uncommon	Trainer			Professor Oak
89/102	Uncommon	Trainer			Revive
90/102	Uncommon	Trainer			Super Potion
91/102	Common	Trainer			Bill
92/102	Common	Trainer			Energy Removal
93/102	Common	Trainer			Gust of Wind
94/102	Common	Trainer			Potion
95/102	Common	Trainer			Switch
96/102	Uncommon	Energy			Double Colorless Energy
97/102		Energy			Fighting Basic Energy
98/102		Energy			Fire Basic Energy
99/102		Energy			Grass Basic Energy
100/102		Energy			Lightning Basic Energy
101/102		Energy			Psychic Basic Energy
102/102		Energy			Water Basic Energy

U.S. COLLECTOR'S GUIDE

"JUNGLE EXPANSION" (SERIES 2)

U.S. SET COMPOSITION

The "Jungle Expansion" is the first "expansion" set of cards released in the U.S. for the Pokémon Trading Card Game. The limited print Jungle expansion was released in June 1999. The unlimited print run cards began selling approximately 2 weeks later (still June 1999).

64 TOTAL CARDS

BY RARITY	
16	Ultra-Rare Holographic
16	Rare (non-Holographic)
16	Uncommon
16	Common

AVAILABLE IN:

"BOOSTER" PACKS:
- $3.29 U.S.
- 11 cards (randomly packaged):
  - 1 Rare / Ultra-Rare cards
  - 3 Uncommon cards
  - 7 Common cards
- When purchased through booster packs, card rarities are distributed as:
  - 1:33 = 3% Ultra-Rare (holographic) cards
  - 2:33 = 6% Rare (non-holographic) cards
  - 9:33 = 27% Uncommon cards
  - 21:33 = 63% Common cards

"THEME" DECKS:
- $9.99 U.S.
- Holographic "Vileplume" paper coin
- 10 damage counters
- "Advanced" Level Rulebook
- 60 cards
- Fixed set of cards (every Theme Deck comes with the following cards):

Water Blast

Pokémon (24)
- (4) Meowth
- (2) Persian
- (4) Eevee
- (1) Vaporeon
- (4) Poliwag
- (2) Poliwhirl
- (1) Seel
- (2) Machop
- (3) Rhyhorn
- (1) Rhydon

Trainer Cards (8)
- (1) Professor Oak
- (2) Gust of Wind
- (1) Switch
- (2) Potion
- (2) Super Potion

Energy (28)
- (14) Water Energy
- (14) Fighting Energy

Power Reserve

Pokémon (23)
- (1) Kangaskhan
- (4) Bellsprout
- (2) Weepinbell
- (2) Oddish
- (1) Gloom
- (4) Nidoran (F)
- (2) Nidorina
- (4) Abra
- (2) Kadabra
- (1) Jynx

Trainer Cards (9)
- (2) Bill
- (3) Potion
- (2) Gust of Wind
- (1) Switch
- (1) Pokédex

Energy (28)
- (17) Grass Energy
- (11) Psychic Energy

64-CARD "JUNGLE" EXPANSION SET

1st Edition released June 1999
Unlimited print run released July 1999

CARD	RARITY	COLOR	LEVEL	NUM	NAME
1/64	Holographic	Colorless	lv 34	#36	Clefable
2/64	Holographic	Lightning	lv 42	#101	Electrode
3/64	Holographic	Fire	lv 28	#136	Flareon
4/64	Holographic	Lightning	lv 29	#135	Jolteon
5/64	Holographic	Colorless	lv 40	#115	Kangaskhan
6/64	Holographic	Psychic	lv 28	#122	Mr. Mime
7/64	Holographic	Grass	lv 43	#31	Nidoqueen
8/64	Holographic	Colorless	lv 40	#18	Pidgeot
9/64	Holographic	Grass	lv 24	#127	Pinsir
10/64	Holographic	Grass	lv 25	#123	Scyther
11/64	Holographic	Colorless	lv 20	#143	Snorlax
12/64	Holographic	Water	lv 42	#134	Vaporeon
13/64	Holographic	Grass	lv 28	#49	Venomoth
14/64	Holographic	Grass	lv 42	#71	Victreebel
15/64	Holographic	Grass	lv 35	#45	Vileplume
16/64	Holographic	Colorless	lv 36	#40	Wigglytuff
17/64	Rare	Colorless	lv 34	#36	Clefable
18/64	Rare	Lightning	lv 42	#101	Electrode
19/64	Rare	Fire	lv 28	#136	Flareon
20/64	Rare	Lightning	lv 29	#135	Jolteon
21/64	Rare	Colorless	lv 40	#115	Kangaskhan
22/64	Rare	Psychic	lv 28	#122	Mr. Mime
23/64	Rare	Grass	lv 43	#031	Nidoqueen
24/64	Rare	Colorless	lv 40	#018	Pidgeot
25/64	Rare	Grass	lv 24	#127	Pinsir
26/64	Rare	Grass	lv 25	#123	Scyther
27/64	Rare	Colorless	lv 20	#143	Snorlax
28/64	Rare	Water	lv 42	#134	Vaporeon
29/64	Rare	Grass	lv 28	#049	Venomoth
30/64	Rare	Grass	lv 42	#071	Victreebel
31/64	Rare	Grass	lv 35	#045	Vileplume
32/64	Rare	Colorless	lv 36	#040	Wigglytuff
33/64	Uncommon	Grass	lv 28	#012	Butterfree
34/64	Uncommon	Colorless	lv 28	#085	Dodrio
35/64	Uncommon	Grass	lv 35	#103	Exeggutor
36/64	Uncommon	Colorless	lv 27	#022	Fearow
37/64	Uncommon	Grass	lv 22	#044	Gloom
38/64	Uncommon	Colorless	lv 26	#108	Lickitung
39/64	Uncommon	Fighting	lv 26	#105	Marowak
40/64	Uncommon	Grass	lv 24	#030	Nidorina

CARD	RARITY	COLOR	LEVEL	NUM	NAME
41/64	Uncommon	Grass	lv 28	#047	Parasect
42/64	Uncommon	Colorless	lv 25	#053	Persian
43/64	Uncommon	Fighting	lv 35	#057	Primeape
44/64	Uncommon	Fire	lv 33	#078	Rapidash
45/64	Uncommon	Fighting	lv 48	#112	Rhydon
46/64	Uncommon	Water	lv 28	#119	Seaking
47/64	Uncommon	Colorless	lv 32	#128	Tauros
48/64	Uncommon	Grass	lv 28	#070	Weepinbell
49/64	Common	Grass	lv 11	#069	Bellsprout
50/64	Common	Fighting	lv 13	#104	Cubone
51/64	Common	Colorless	lv 12	#133	Eevee
52/64	Common	Grass	lv 14	#102	Exeggcute
53/64	Common	Water	lv 12	#118	Goldeen
54/64	Common	Colorless	lv 14	#039	Jigglypuff
55/64	Common	Fighting	lv 07	#056	Mankey
56/64	Common	Colorless	lv 15	#052	Meowth
57/64	Common	Grass	lv 13	#029	Nidoran (F)
58/64	Common	Grass	lv 08	#043	Oddish
59/64	Common	Grass	lv 08	#046	Paras
60/64	Common	Lightning	lv 14	#025	Pikachu
61/64	Common	Fighting	lv 18	#111	Rhyhorn
62/64	Common	Colorless	lv 13	#021	Spearow
63/64	Common	Grass	lv 12	#048	Venonat
64/64	Common	Trainer			Poké Ball

MARK ELIES

U.S. COLLECTOR'S GUIDE

"FOSSIL EXPANSION" (SERIES 3)

U.S. SET COMPOSITION

The "Fossil Expansion" is the second "expansion" set of cards released in the U.S. for the Pokémon Trading Card Game. The limited print Fossil expansion was released in September 1999. The unlimited print cards began selling at the exact same time, and in many cases were available in retail a few days prior to the limited print cards.

62
TOTAL
CARDS

AVAILABLE IN:

"BOOSTER" PACKS:

- $3.29 U.S.
- 11 cards (randomly packaged):
  - 1 Rare / Ultra-Rare cards
  - 3 Uncommon cards
  - 7 Common cards
- When purchased through booster packs, card rarities are distributed as:
  - 1:33 = 3% Ultra-Rare (holographic) cards
  - 2:33 = 6% Rare (non-holographic) cards
  - 9:33 = 27% Uncommon cards
  - 21:33 = 63% Common cards

BY RARITY	
15	Ultra-Rare Holographic
15	Rare (non-Holographic)
16	Uncommon
16	Common

"THEME" DECKS:

- $9.99 U.S.
- Holographic "Aerodactyl" paper coin
- 10 damage counters
- "Advanced" Level Rulebook
- 60 cards
- Fixed set of cards (every Theme Deck comes with the following cards):

Bodyguard

Pokémon (23)
- (4) Zubat
- (2) Golbat
- (4) Grimer
- (1) Muk
- (4) Koffing
- (2) Bulbasaur
- (1) Onix
- (3) Geodude
- (2) Graveler

Trainer Cards (9)
- (2) Professor Oak
- (4) Potion
- (2) Super Potion
- (1) Pokémon Center

Energy (28)
- (16) Grass Energy
- (12) Fighting Energy

Lock Down

Pokémon (21)
- (1) Lapras
- (4) Horsea
- (2) Seadra
- (4) Krabby
- (2) Kingler
- (2) Magmar (fossil)
- (3) Ponyta
- (3) Vulpix

Trainer Cards (11)
- (2) Bill
- (2) Potion
- (2) Super Potion
- (2) Switch
- (1) Energy Search
- (1) Gambler
- (1) Full Heal

Energy (28)
- (14) Water Energy
- (14) Fire Energy

64-CARD "FOSSIL" EXPANSION SET

1st Edition released September 1999
Unlimited print run released September 1999

CARD	RARITY	COLOR	LEVEL	NUM	NAME
1/62	Holographic	Fighting	Lv28	#142	Aerodactyl
2/62	Holographic	Water	Lv35	#144	Articuno
3/62	Holographic	Colorless	Lv20	#132	Ditto
4/62	Holographic	Colorless	Lv45	#149	Dragonite
5/62	Holographic	Psychic	Lv38	#094	Gengar
6/62	Holographic	Psychic	Lv17	#093	Haunter
7/62	Holographic	Fighting	Lv30	#106	Hitmonlee
8/62	Holographic	Psychic	Lv36	#097	Hypno
9/62	Holographic	Fighting	Lv30	#141	Kabutops
10/62	Holographic	Water	Lv31	#131	Lapras
11/62	Holographic	Lightning	Lv35	#082	Magneton
12/62	Holographic	Fire	Lv35	#146	Moltres
13/62	Holographic	Grass	Lv34	#089	Muk
14/62	Holographic	Lightning	Lv45	#026	Raichu
15/62	Holographic	Lightning	Lv40	#145	Zapdos
16/62	Rare	Fighting	Lv28	#142	Aerodactyl
17/62	Rare	Water	Lv35	#144	Articuno
18/62	Rare	Colorless	Lv20	#132	Ditto
19/62	Rare	Colorless	Lv45	#149	Dragonite
20/62	Rare	Psychic	Lv38	#094	Gengar
21/62	Rare	Psychic	Lv17	#093	Haunter
22/62	Rare	Fighting	Lv30	#106	Hitmonlee
23/62	Rare	Psychic	Lv36	#097	Hypno
24/62	Rare	Fighting	Lv30	#141	Kabutops
25/62	Rare	Water	Lv31	#131	Lapras
26/62	Rare	Lightning	Lv35	#082	Magneton
27/62	Rare	Fire	Lv35	#146	Moltres
28/62	Rare	Grass	Lv34	#089	Muk
29/62	Rare	Lightning	Lv45	#026	Raichu
30/62	Rare	Lightning	Lv40	#145	Zapdos
31/62	Uncommon	Grass	Lv27	#024	Arbok
32/62	Uncommon	Water	Lv25	#091	Cloyster
33/62	Uncommon	Psychic	Lv17	#092	Gastly
34/62	Uncommon	Grass	Lv29	#042	Golbat
35/62	Uncommon	Water	Lv27	#055	Golduck
36/62	Uncommon	Fighting	Lv36	#076	Golem
37/62	Uncommon	Fighting	Lv29	#075	Graveller
38/62	Uncommon	Water	Lv27	#099	Kingler
39/62	Uncommon	Fire	Lv31	#126	Magmar
40/62	Uncommon	Water	Lv32	#139	Omastar

CARD	RARITY	COLOR	LEVEL	NUM	NAME
41/62	Uncommon	Fighting	Lv33	#028	Sandslash
42/62	Uncommon	Water	Lv23	#117	Seadra
43/62	Uncommon	Psychic	Lv26	#080	Slowbro
44/62	Uncommon	Water	Lv21	#073	Tentacruel
45/62	Uncommon	Grass	Lv27	#110	Weezing
46/62	Common	Grass	Lv10	#023	Ekans
47/62	Common	Fighting	Lv16	#074	Geodude
48/62	Common	Grass	Lv17	#088	Grimer
49/62	Common	Water	Lv19	#116	Horsea
50/62	Common	Fighting	Lv09	#140	Kabuto
51/62	Common	Water	Lv20	#098	Krabby
52/62	Common	Water	Lv19	#138	Omanyte
53/62	Common	Water	Lv15	#054	Psyduck
54/62	Common	Water	Lv08	#090	Shellder
55/62	Common	Psychic	Lv18	#079	Slowpoke
56/62	Common	Water	Lv10	#072	Tentacool
57/62	Common	Grass	Lv10	#041	Zubat
58/62	Uncommon	Trainer			Old Man Fuji
59/62	Common	Trainer			Energy Transfer
60/62	Common	Trainer			Gambler
61/62	Common	Trainer			Recycle
62/62	Common	Trainer			Mysterious Fossil

MARK ELIES

Pokémon TCG Fossil Expansion Player's Guide

POCKET MONSTERS COLLECTOR'S GUIDE

It's no surprise that the Pokémon Trading Card Game has been received so incredibly well here in the United States. The invasion was well planned and thoroughly researched—in Japan! As early as 1996, the Japanese version of the Pokémon TCG (titled "Pocket Monsters Card Game" over there) was in full swing. The hysteria that has accompanied the game on the North American continent is old-hat for the island nation that created and fostered the game.

Coast has implemented a few production and marketing changes. Many of these changes are universally accepted as beneficial to the hobby—Set numbering on every card, the creation of numerous Pre-Constructed Theme Decks for each set, and the release of basic energy cards in Base set booster packs. However, Wizards has also been linked with a few changes that remain controversial for both players and collectors alike—Decreased odds of obtaining Base set holographic cards, introduction of non-holographic rare cards in Jungle and Fossil, and withholding a key card (Mew) from the Fossil expansion.

The Same Game

Every single aspect of Wizards of the Coast's Pokémon Trading Card Game has been duplicated as a direct translation from the original Japanese card game. Everything from Pokémon Hit Points and Retreat Costs to Weakness and Resistance are identical. Attack moves and Pokémon Powers now have English names, but their functionality is unchanged. Even the artwork on the Japanese cards was left untouched. This is no surprise based on the Japanese game's success and further illustrates the axiom: "If it ain't broke, don't fix it".

Although card functionality and game mechanics weren't touched, Wizards of the

Accepted Changes to the Game

The lack of "set numbering" on Japanese Pocket Monster cards makes them difficult to keep track of. The U.S. cards all show a "card number" (next to a number identifying the set size), in the lower right-hand corner. From this you immediately know how many, and which numbered cards you may be missing from your U.S. collection. The Japanese cards are a bit more difficult, but we've tried to make the set collection process easy for you with this strategy guide. Each of the Japanese set lists in this book show all of the unique identifying information you will need in order to complete your collections—Pokémon Name, Pokémon Number, and Pokémon Level. Creatures has been very careful to keep functionally different versions of each monster's cards identified with different Pokémon Levels. Use this information to correctly identify Japanese Pokémon cards in the set lists.

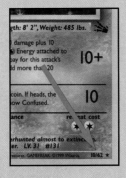 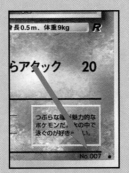

It is actually a misrepresentation to refer to Japanese Base set decks as "Starter decks". You certainly wouldn't want to "start" learning the game with only one of these decks to assist you. They are packaged with random cards from the Base set with a smattering of every color of energy card to boot. In many cases, Pokémon evolutions will appear in Base set decks without the appropriate Basic Pokémon to go along. This makes for an unplayable deck. However, since these decks are the only source for basic energy cards in the Japanese card game, players will typically find themselves needing multiple copies of them in order to build playable decks. This could get expensive after a time, and Wizard's dedication to filling Base set booster slots with energy cards should be appreciated here.

Controversial Changes to the Game

It doesn't take long strolling through the internet or at a local hobby/game store to realize that Americans are spending a LOT of money on Wizard's Pokémon cards. The random nature of the booster packs and the rar-

ity scheme help fuel this fire. These collectible aspects of Trading Card Games are like a double-edged sword; They inflate the value of the cards by limiting the availability to the most desirable ones. But, in the United States, this availability is reduced significantly from the original release of the card game in Japan. Japanese Base set booster packs were produced with approximately one out of every TWO packs containing a holographic rare card, but Wizard of the Coast's Base set holographics are released as one out of every THREE booster packs. Poke-maniacs in the U.S. need to purchase at least 50% more Base set booster packs to obtain the same number of holographic cards as Japanese collectors. And in the Jungle and Fossil expansions, Japanese packs include a holographic card in every single pack! There are no non-holographic copies of the rare cards as there are in the English boosters. This means that English card collectors will be buying at least 3 times the number of U.S. packs as Japanese collectors have purchased to finish card sets.

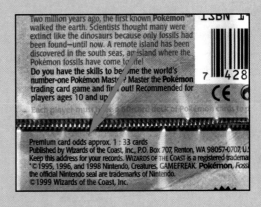

Contentious issues always seem to have both upsides and downsides. Advocates of Wizard's policy towards ultra-rare holographic cards will readily point to the increased value of their collections as basis enough to decrease holographic availability. Along with this, the special "Edition 1" stamp that the first print run of U.S. cards contain help satisfy the collector's need to maintain value. At the same time, limited print-run product and functionally equivalent non-holographic rares assist the game player's need to obtain more cards. The "non-player collectors" should be more focused onto "Edition 1" products and less prone to snatch up all the available unlimited print run cards necessary to build decks and play

Transform Pokémon. L

games. Collectors and Players can work together to best promote the needs of each other, and make the most out of their Pokémon TCG collections.

Pocket Monster Card Game Background

The Pokémon Game Boy game was the brain child of Tsunekazu Tajiri, founder and designer for the software gaming company Game Freak. As Game Boy Poke-mania swept Japan and licenses for new products and games were being devised, Tajiri turned to Creatures' president Tsunekazu Ishihara to develop the Pocket Monsters Card Game. Creatures is the Japanese game company who worked with Pokémon's creator to generate artwork for all 151 of the original monsters.

Ishihara's long time involvement with Tajiri and the rest of the Pokémon development team allowed the design of a card game that is instinctively rooted in the original Game Boy cartridges. There are so many features to the Nintendo cartridges to work with, it was a massive task to streamline the essence of Pokémon battle for the card game, but this is exactly what Ishihara has remarkably accomplished. And not only does the card game reflect all the best aspects of Pokémon battle in the Game Boy games, it goes well-beyond the cartridges by providing significant advances in attack moves and Pokémon Trainer involvement. Pokémon was designed by gamers, for gamers, and the Pokémon universe has defi-

nitely evolved into a more strategic and game oriented realm with the creation of the collectible card game.

Once designed, Creatures called upon another company to manufacture and distribute the card game—Media Factory in Tokyo. Together, they have been able to keep revitalizing the market with new Pocket Monster Card Game products on a frequent basis. There are currently 15 different full sets of cards that are still available in retail. Everything from Base set "Starter" decks to the newest major expansion set: "Challenge from the Darkness — Gym Expansion #2". And each new release of cards introduces all new attack moves and mechanics, further broadening the combinations with which the TCG player can work with.

Media Factory Product Guide

Base Set (Boosters/Starter Decks) . . . . .Fall 1996
Jungle Expansion . . . . .Spring 1997
Fossil Expansion . . . . .Summer 1997
Team Rocket Expansion . . . . .Fall 1997
Vending Machine Sets . . . . .Winter 1997
Gym Leader Decks (Brock/Misty) . . . . .Spring 1998
Gym Leader Decks (Lt. Surge/Erika) . .Summer 1998
Gym Leaders Expansion #1 . . . . .Fall 1998
Gym Leader Decks
    (Blaine & Sabrina) . . . . Spring 1999
Gym Leaders Expansion #2 . . . . . . .Summer 1999

Pokémon TCG Fossil Expansion Player's Guide

In addition to the full sets periodically released, there have also been special promotional cards given away at unique events or distributed with specialized merchandise. Promo cards have accompanied everything from comic books and magazines to calendars and music CDs. Two recent movie releases in Japan were celebrated with promotional Pocket Monster cards. "Revelation Lugia" was the newest full-length Pokémon feature movie in Japan during 1999 and a special promo card (Ancient Mew) was given away at the first showings during the summer. Also, "Pikachu's Summer Vacation" (an animated short that was subsequently released in the U.S. in November 1999) brought 18 new promo cards to Japanese movie customers. These "Southern Islands" promo cards were sold in 6 different fixed set packages of 3 cards each, and every package contained a holographic card (including some of the "unnumbered" new monsters that won't be released in Game Boy games until Gold/Silver is released)! There is even a very exclusive "flying Pikachu" promo card that you can only obtain by taking an ANA (All-Nippon-Airways) international flight on one of this companies Pokémon Boeing 747 Jumbo Jets! (An international airfare ticket is perhaps the ONLY product that may actually cost more than what the promotional Pocket Monster card will fetch on the card-singles market!)

In addition to game cards, there are also many cool card game accessories that have evolved over time. Media Factory is right in tune with its card game players and has a whole line up of merchandise to make the most of every Trainer's battles. For beginning players they offer "intro packs" with good, playable decks and instructional video cassettes that teach the game. As you can guess, these intro decks are designed for the most efficient learning curve to mastering the game. Beyond simple introductions however, Media Factory offers hard plastic organizing boxes and deck boxes, branded "Pocket Monsters Card Game" card sleeves, special damage counters and poison markers, and a 2-player felt table mat to run your match on. These official PMCG products are must-haves for serious players who want to treat their cards with respect and care. After all, Pokémon Trainers are judged on how kindly they treat their Pokémon.

A Monster Success

The Pocket Monsters Card Game may be primarily a kid's game in Japan, but these kids are taken extremely seriously! Media Factory organizes and sponsors major national tournaments for kids from all over the island. After regional qualifying tournaments, players are given an all-expense paid trip to the location of that season's ultimate battle. With commentated television coverage and massive bronzed Pokémon statues to the victors, Japanese Pocket Monster Card Game tournaments are world-class events and a big attraction. Although it doesn't have a built-in Water Gun attack, one of these Blastoise statues would certainly cement a player's status among Pokemaniacs as a Pokémon Master.

With well over 1 billion cards already sold, the Pocket Monsters Card Game can clearly be labeled as a phenomenal success. Even with the reports trickling in about Pocket Monster's hysteria losing some steam in Japan, the U.S. has just begun its journey up the ramp of Poke-mania. With less than one quarter of the existing Japanese cards currently translated into English, this means nothing but good things for those of us with a passion for a good Pokémon match.

"BASIC SET" or "STARTER SET" (SERIES 1)

JAPANESE SET COMPOSITION

The PMCG "Basic Set" is the first 102 card set released in Japan. It includes Japanese equivalents (duplicating everything from card attributes, abilities, art, and rarity) of every card released in Wizards of the Coast's "Base" set of cards.

AVAILABLE IN:

"Starter" Decks:
- 1300 Yen (approximately $19.00 as an import)
- 60 cards
- Random cards (not fixed like U.S. "Starter" Decks)
- Basic Energy Cards included
- Durable Plastic holographic foil "Chansey" coin included
- Japanese Rulebooks included

"Booster" Packs:
- 291 Yen (approximately $4.00 as an import)
- 10 cards
  - 1 Rare: 1 in 2 chance of getting a rare holographic
  - 3 Uncommon
  - 6 Common
  - no Basic Energy cards

102 TOTAL CARDS

BY RARITY

16	Rare Holographic
16	Rare
32	Uncommon
32	Common
6	Basic Energy (no rarity)

BY TYPE

1 Special Energy Card (Double-Colorless Energy)
6 Basic Energy Cards
26 Trainer Cards
69 Pokémon Cards:

13 Grass:
- 6 Basic Pokémon
- 4 Stage 1 Evolutions
- 3 Stage 2 Evolutions

9 Fire:
- 5 Basic Pokémon
- 3 Stage 1 Evolutions
- 1 Stage 2 Evolution

8 Lightning:
- 5 Basic Pokémon
- 3 Stage 1 Evolutions

12 Water:
- 5 Basic Pokémon
- 5 Stage 1 Evolutions
- 2 Stage 2 Evolutions

8 Psychic:
- 5 Basic Pokémon
- 2 Stage 1 Evolutions
- 1 Stage 2 Evolution

8 Fighting:
- 5 Basic Pokémon
- 2 Stage 1 Evolutions
- 1 Stage 2 Evolution

11 Colorless:
- 8 Basic Pokémon
- 3 Stage 1 Evolutions

Note: *Description* and *Name* will be english equivalents.
Lists are sorted to match the Media Factory (Japanese) Card List ("color" first, then "pokémon number")

FULL CARD LIST

(Rarity) (Color) Description: Name	(Rarity) (Color) Description: Name
(C) (G) Lv13 #001: Bulbasaur	(U) (P) Lv23 #124: Jynx
(U) (G) Lv20 #002: Ivysaur	(H) (P) Lv53 #150: Mewtwo
(H) (G) Lv67 #003: Venusaur	(C) (F) Lv12 #027: Sandshrew
(C) (G) Lv13 #010: Caterpie	(C) (F) Lv08 #050: Diglett
(C) (G) Lv21 #011: Metapod	(R) (F) Lv36 #051: Dugtrio
(C) (G) Lv12 #013: Weedle	(C) (F) Lv20 #066: Machop
(U) (G) Lv23 #014: Kakuna	(U) (F) Lv40 #067: Machoke
(R) (G) Lv32 #015: Beedrill	(H) (F) Lv67 #068: Machamp
(C) (G) Lv20 #032: Nidoran(M)	(C) (F) Lv12 #095: Onix
(U) (G) Lv25 #033: Nidorino	(H) (F) Lv33 #107: Hitmonchan
(H) (G) Lv48 #034: Nidoking	(C) (C) Lv08 #016: Pidgey
(C) (G) Lv13 #109: Koffing	(R) (C) Lv36 #017: Pidgeotto
(C) (G) Lv08 #114: Tangela	(C) (C) Lv09 #019: Rattata
(C) (R) Lv10 #004: Charmander	(U) (C) Lv41 #020: Raticate
(U) (R) Lv32 #005: Charmeleon	(H) (C) Lv14 #035: Clefairy
(H) (R) Lv76 #006: Charizard	(U) (C) Lv20 #083: Farfetch'd
(C) (R) Lv11 #037: Vulpix	(C) (C) Lv10 #084: Doduo
(H) (R) Lv32 #038: Ninetales	(H) (C) Lv55 #113: Chansey
(U) (R) Lv18 #058: Growlithe	(U) (C) Lv12 #137: Porygon
(U) (R) Lv45 #059: Arcanine	(U) (C) Lv10 #147: Dratini
(C) (R) Lv10 #077: Ponyta	(R) (C) Lv33 #148: Dragonair
(U) (R) Lv24 #126: Magmar	(U) (T) Trainer: Professor Oak
(C) (W) Lv08 #007: Squirtle	(R) (T) Trainer: Impostor Professor Oak
(U) (W) Lv22 #008: Wartortle	(C) (T) Trainer: Bill
(H) (W) Lv52 #009: Blastoise	(R) (T) Trainer: Lass
(C) (W) Lv13 #060: Poliwag	(R) (T) Trainer: Pokémon Trader
(U) (W) Lv28 #061: Poliwhirl	(R) (T) Trainer: Pokémon Breeder
(H) (W) Lv48 #062: Poliwrath	(R) (T) Trainer: Clefairy Doll
(U) (W) Lv12 #086: Seel	(U) (T) Trainer: Energy Retrieval
(U) (W) Lv42 #087: Dewgong	(C) (T) Trainer: Energy Removal
(C) (W) Lv15 #120: Staryu	(R) (T) Trainer: Super Energy Removal
(C) (W) Lv28 #121: Starmie	(C) (T) Trainer: Switch
(U) (W) Lv08 #129: Magikarp	(U) (T) Trainer: Pokémon Center
(H) (W) Lv41 #130: Gyarados	(R) (T) Trainer: Scoop Up
(C) (L) Lv12 #025: Pikachu	(R) (T) Trainer: Computer Search
(H) (L) Lv40 #026: Raichu	(U) (T) Trainer: Pokédex
(C) (L) Lv13 #081: Magnemite	(U) (T) Trainer: PlusPower
(H) (L) Lv28 #082: Magneton	(U) (T) Trainer: Defender
(C) (L) Lv10 #100: Voltorb	(R) (T) Trainer: Item Finder
(R) (L) Lv40 #101: Electrode	(C) (T) Trainer: Gust of Wind
(R) (L) Lv35 #125: Electabuzz	(R) (T) Trainer: Devolution Spray
(H) (L) Lv64 #145: Zapdos	(U) (T) Trainer: Revive
(C) (P) Lv10 #063: Abra	(U) (T) Trainer: Super Potion
(U) (P) Lv38 #064: Kadabra	(C) (T) Trainer: Potion
(H) (P) Lv42 #065: Alakazam	(U) (T) Trainer: Full Heal
(C) (P) Lv08 #092: Gastly	(U) (T) Trainer: Maintenance
(U) (P) Lv22 #093: Haunter	(U) (T) Trainer: Pokémon Flute
(C) (P) Lv12 #096: Drowzee	(U) (E) Energy: Double Colorless Energy

"Color": R=Fire, F=Fight, G=Grass, P=Psychic, W=Water, L=Lightning, C=Colorless, T=Trainer, E=Energy
Rarity: H=Holographic (Foil), R=Rare (non-Foil), U=Uncommon, C=Common, N=non-designated (basic energy)

"JUNGLE EXPANSION" (SERIES 2)

JAPANESE SET COMPOSITION

The "Jungle Expansion" is the first expansion set of PMCG cards released in Japan. It includes Japanese equivalents (duplicating everything from card attributes, abilities, art, and rarity) of almost every card released in Wizards of the Coast's "Jungle Expansion" set of cards. The Japanese Jungle Expansion did not include non-holographic versions of the foil rare cards. This makes the Japanese set smaller (48 cards) and holographic rares much easier to obtain.

48 TOTAL CARDS

AVAILABLE IN:
"Booster" Packs:
- 291 Yen (approximately $4.00 as an import)
- 10 cards
  - 1 Rare: (always a holographic foil)
  - 3 Uncommon
  - 6 Common
  - no Basic Energy cards

BY RARITY
16	Rare (Foil)
16	Uncommon
16	Common

BY TYPE

1 Trainer Card
47 Pokémon Cards:
  18 Grass:
    8 Basic Pokémon
    6 Stage 1 Evolutions
    4 Stage 2 Evolutions
  3 Water:
    1 Basic Pokémon
    2 Stage 1 Evolutions
  3 Lightning:
    1 Basic Pokémon
    2 Stage 1 Evolutions

2 Fire:
  2 Stage 1 Evolutions
1 Psychic:
  1 Basic Pokémon
6 Fighting:
  3 Basic Pokémon
  3 Stage 1 Evolutions
14 Colorless:
  8 Basic Pokémon
  5 Stage 1 Evolutions
  1 Stage 2 Evolutions

Note: *Description* and *Name* will be english equivalents.

This list is sorted to match the Media Factory (Japanese) Card List ("color" first, then "pokémon number")

FULL CARD LIST

(Rarity) (Color) Description: Name	(Rarity) (Color) Description: Name
(U) (G) Lv28 #012: Butterfree	(H) (L) Lv42 #101: Electrode
(C) (G) Lv13 #029: Nidoran(F)	(H) (L) Lv29 #135: Jolteon
(U) (G) Lv24 #030: Nidorina	(H) (P) Lv28 #122: Mr.Mime
(H) (G) Lv43 #031: Nidoqueen	(C) (F) Lv07 #056: Mankey
(C) (G) Lv08 #043: Oddish	(U) (F) Lv35 #057: Primeape
(U) (G) Lv22 #044: Gloom	(C) (F) Lv13 #104: Cubone
(H) (G) Lv35 #045: Vileplume	(U) (F) Lv26 #105: Marowak
(C) (G) Lv08 #046: Paras	(C) (F) Lv18 #111: Rhyhorn
(U) (G) Lv28 #047: Parasect	(U) (F) Lv48 #112: Rhydon
(C) (G) Lv12 #048: Venonat	(H) (C) Lv40 #018: Pidgeot
(H) (G) Lv28 #049: Venomoth	(C) (C) Lv13 #021: Spearow
(C) (G) Lv11 #069: Bellsprout	(U) (C) Lv27 #022: Fearow
(U) (G) Lv28 #070: Weepinbell	(H) (C) Lv34 #036: Clefable
(H) (G) Lv42 #071: Victreebel	(C) (C) Lv14 #039: Jigglypuff
(C) (G) Lv14 #102: Exeggcute	(H) (C) Lv36 #040: Wigglytuff
(U) (G) Lv35 #103: Exeggutor	(C) (C) Lv15 #052: Meowth
(H) (G) Lv25 #123: Scyther	(U) (C) Lv25 #053: Persian
(H) (G) Lv24 #127: Pinsir	(U) (C) Lv28 #085: Dodrio
(U) (R) Lv33 #078: Rapidash	(U) (C) Lv26 #108: Lickitung
(H) (R) Lv28 #136: Flareon	(H) (C) Lv40 #115: Kangaskhan
(C) (W) Lv12 #118: Goldeen	(U) (C) Lv32 #128: Tauros
(U) (W) Lv28 #119: Seaking	(C) (C) Lv12 #133: Eevee
(H) (W) Lv42 #134: Vaporeon	(H) (C) Lv20 #143: Snorlax
(C) (L) Lv14 #025: Pikachu	(C) (T) Trainer: "PokéBall"

"Color": R=Fire, F=Fight, G=Grass, P=Psychic, W=Water, L=Lightning, C=Colorless, T=Trainer, E=Energy
Rarity: H=Holographic (Foil), R=Rare (non-Foil), U=Uncommon, C=Common, N=non-designated (basic energy)

"FOSSIL EXPANSION" (SERIES 3)

JAPANESE SET COMPOSITION

The "Fossil Expansion" is the second expansion set of PMCG cards released in Japan. It includes Japanese equivalents (duplicating everything from card attributes, abilities, art, and rarity) of almost every card released in Wizards of the Coast's "Fossil Expansion" set of cards. The Japanese Fossil Expansion did not include non-holographic versions of the foil rare cards. Also, the Japanese Fossil Expansion included an additional rare card — Pokémon #151 Mew. Together this makes the Japanese set smaller (48 cards) and holographic rares much easier to obtain than the U.S. set.

48 TOTAL CARDS

AVAILABLE IN:
"Booster" Packs:
- 291 Yen (approximately $4.00 as an import)
- 10 cards
    - 1 Rare: (always a holographic foil)
    - 3 Uncommon
    - 6 Common
    - no Basic Energy cards

BY RARITY
16 Rare (Foil)
16 Uncommon
16 Common

BY TYPE

5 Trainer Card
43 Pokémon Cards:
   7 Grass:
      3 Basic Pokémon
      4 Stage 1 Evolutions
   14 Water:
      7 Basic Pokémon
      6 Stage 1 Evolutions
      1 Stage 2 Evolutions
   7 Psychic:
      3 Basic Pokémon
      3 Stage 1 Evolutions
      1 Stage 2 Evolutions

3 Lightning:
   1 Basic Pokémon
   2 Stage 1 Evolutions
2 Fire:
   2 Basic Pokémon
8 Fighting:
   2 Basic Pokémon
   4 Stage 1 Evolutions
   2 Stage 2 Evolutions
2 Colorless:
   1 Basic Pokémon
   1 Stage 2 Evolutions

Note: *Description* and *Name* will be english equivalents.
This list is sorted to match the Media Factory (Japanese) Card List ("color" first, then "pokémon number")

FULL CARD LIST

(Rarity) (Color) Description: Name	(Rarity) (Color) Description: Name
(C) (G) Lv10 #023: Ekans	(H) (L) Lv35 #082: Magneton
(U) (G) Lv27 #024: Arbok	(H) (L) Lv40 #145: Zapdos
(C) (G) Lv10 #041: Zubat	(C) (P) Lv18 #079: Slowpoke
(U) (G) Lv29 #042: Golbat	(U) (P) Lv26 #080: Slowbro
(C) (G) Lv17 #088: Grimer	(U) (P) Lv17 #092: Gastly
(H) (G) Lv34 #089: Muk	(H) (P) Lv17 #093: Haunter
(U) (G) Lv27 #110: Weezing	(H) (P) Lv38 #094: Gengar
(U) (R) Lv31 #126: Magmar	(H) (P) Lv36 #097: Hypno
(H) (R) Lv35 #146: Moltres	(H) (P) Lv23 #151: Mew
(C) (W) Lv15 #054: Psyduck	(U) (F) Lv33 #028: Sandslash
(U) (W) Lv27 #055: Golduck	(C) (F) Lv16 #074: Geodude
(C) (W) Lv10 #072: Tentacool	(U) (F) Lv29 #075: Graveller
(U) (W) Lv21 #073: Tentacruel	(U) (F) Lv36 #076: Golem
(C) (W) Lv08 #090: Shellder	(H) (F) Lv30 #106: Hitmonlee
(U) (W) Lv25 #091: Cloyster	(C) (F) Lv09 #140: Kabuto
(C) (W) Lv20 #098: Krabby	(H) (F) Lv30 #141: Kabutops
(U) (W) Lv27 #099: Kingler	(H) (F) Lv28 #142: Aerodactyl
(C) (W) Lv19 #116: Horsea	(H) (C) Lv20 #132: Ditto
(U) (W) Lv23 #117: Seadra	(H) (C) Lv45 #149: Dragonite
(H) (W) Lv31 #131: Lapras	(U) (T) Trainer: "Fuji Old Man"
(C) (W) Lv19 #138: Omanyte	(C) (T) Trainer: "Fossil"
(U) (W) Lv32 #139: Omastar	(C) (T) Trainer: "Energy Search"
(H) (W) Lv35 #144: Articuno	(C) (T) Trainer: "Gambler"
(H) (L) Lv45 #026: Raichu	(C) (T) Trainer: "Recycle"

"Color": R=Fire, F=Fight, G=Grass, P=Psychic, W=Water, L=Lightning, C=Colorless, T=Trainer, E=Energy
Rarity: H=Holographic (Foil), R=Rare (non-Foil), U=Uncommon, C=Common, N=non-designated (basic energy)

"TEAM ROCKET EXPANSION" (SERIES 4) v2.0

JAPANESE SET COMPOSITION

The "Team Rocket Expansion" is the third expansion set of PMCG cards released in Japan. At the time of this printing, it has an expected North American release date of May 2000.

65 TOTAL CARDS

AVAILABLE IN:
"Booster" Packs:
- 291 Yen (approximately $4.00 as an import)
- 10 cards
    - 1 Rare: (always a holographic foil)
    - 3 Uncommon
    - 6 Common
    - no Basic Energy cards

BY RARITY

1	Super Rare (Foil)
16	Rare (Foil)
16	Uncommon
32	Common

NOTE: One of the rare cards from this set is included in booster packs in apparently a smaller distribution than other holographic rare cards. The "Here Come the Rockets!" trainer card is referred to as "super-rare" card and has a white star for a rarity symbol instead of the normal black star. Although we could not find actual distribution statistics from Media Factory, the author's personal experience yielded 1 of these cards in 60 booster packs. For a set of only 16 holographic rare cards, this is well below the average quantity that should be seen if "Here Come the Rockets!" was distributed at the same frequency.

BY TYPE

3 Energy Cards
9 Trainer Cards
53 Pokémon Cards:
   11 Grass:
      5 Basic Pokémon
      5 Stage 1 Evolutions
      1 Stage 2 Evolutions
   6 Fire:
      2 Basic Pokémon
      3 Stage 1 Evolutions
      1 Stage 2 Evolutions
   8 Water:
      3 Basic Pokémon
      4 Stage 1 Evolutions
      1 Stage 2 Evolutions

5 Lightning:
   2 Basic Pokémon
   3 Stage 1 Evolutions
7 Psychic:
   3 Basic Pokémon
   3 Stage 1 Evolutions
   1 Stage 2 Evolutions
7 Fighting:
   3 Basic Pokémon
   3 Stage 1 Evolutions
   1 Stage 2 Evolutions
9 Colorless:
   5 Basic Pokémon
   3 Stage 1 Evolutions
   1 Stage 2 Evolutions

Note: *Description* and *Name* will be **english equivalents**.
This list is sorted to match the Media Factory (Japanese) Card List ("color" first, then "pokémon number")

CHARMANDER (Lv09)
CARD NUMBER: 004
RARITY: Common
NOTES: Pokémon Power: Take a Fire Energy card from benched Pokémon and use it on Charmander.

"BAD" CHARMELEON (Lv23)
CARD NUMBER: 005
RARITY: Uncommon
NOTES: Second attack does 70 damage, but you must flip a coin and risk losing a Fire Energy card.

"BAD" CHARIZARD (Lv38)
CARD NUMBER: 006
RARITY: Holofoil
NOTES: Second attack: Flip coin for each Fire Energy card attached to do 50x number of heads, then discard Fire cards.

SQUIRTLE (Lv16)
CARD NUMBER: 007
RARITY: Common

"BAD" WARTORTLE (Lv21)
CARD NUMBER: 008
RARITY: Uncommon
NOTES: Second attack: If Wartortle is damaged next turn, same damage done to opponent.

"BAD" BLASTOISE (Lv28)
CARD NUMBER: 009
RARITY: Holofoil
NOTES: Second attack: Does 10 damage to Blastoise, too. Flip a coin, if heads, no damage to Blastoise next turn.

RATTATA (Lv12)
CARD NUMBER: 019
RARITY: Common
NOTES: Pokémon Power: Swap side card with top card of deck.

"BAD" RATICATE (Lv25)
CARD NUMBER: 020
RARITY: Common
NOTES: Second attack: Flip a coin, if tails, attack fails.

EKANS (Lv15)
CARD NUMBER: 023
RARITY: Common
NOTES: Second attack: Flip a coin, if heads, opponent gets poisoned.

"BAD" ARBOK (Lv25)
CARD NUMBER: 024
RARITY: Holofoil
NOTES: Second attack: poisons opponent, plus 10 damage to all benched Pokémon, regardless of defenses.

ZUBAT (Lv09)
CARD NUMBER: 041
RARITY: Common

"BAD" GOLBAT (Lv25)
CARD NUMBER: 042
RARITY: Holofoil
NOTES: Pokémon Power: When placed on bench, can bite any opponent benched Pokémon for 10 damage.

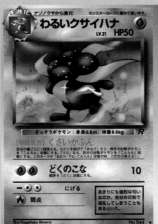

ODDISH (Lv21)
CARD NUMBER: 043
RARITY: Common

"BAD" GLOOM (Lv21)
CARD NUMBER: 044
RARITY: Uncommon
NOTES: Pokémon Power: Flip coin, if heads, opponent active Pokémon is confused, if tails, you are.

"BAD" VILEPLUME (Lv29)
CARD NUMBER: 045
RARITY: Holofoil
NOTES: Pokémon Power: When this card is in play, no Trainer cards can be used by either player.

DIGLETT (Lv15)
CARD NUMBER: 050
RARITY: Common
NOTES: First attack causes 20 damage to any of opponent's visible Pokémon.

"BAD" DUGTRIO (Lv18)
CARD NUMBER: 051
RARITY: Holofoil
NOTES: Pokémon Power: When opponent tries to retreat Pokémon, they must flip coin. If tails, 20 damage.

MEOWTH (Lv10)
CARD NUMBER: 052
RARITY: Common
NOTES: Attack: Flip a coin, if heads, cause 20 damage to any visible Pokémon.

"BAD" PERSIAN (Lv28)
CARD NUMBER: 053
RARITY: Common
NOTES: First attack: Flip a coin, if heads, choose opponent benched Pokémon to switch with active Pokémon.

PSYDUCK (Lv16)
CARD NUMBER: 054
RARITY: Common
NOTES: First attack allows you to draw a card from your deck.

"BAD" GOLDUCK (Lv23)
CARD NUMBER: 055
RARITY: Uncommon
NOTES: First attack: Trash one energy card to draw three cards from deck.

MANKEY (Lv14)
CARD NUMBER: 056
RARITY: Common
NOTES: First attack: Shuffle opponent's deck.

"BAD" PRIMEAPE (Lv23)
CARD NUMBER: 057
RARITY: Uncommon
NOTES: Pokémon Power: When confused, can do additional 30 damage.

ABRA (Lv14)
CARD NUMBER: 063
RARITY: Common
NOTES: First attack: Remove all damage, trash attached cards, and shuffle Abra back into deck (Disappear).

"BAD" KADABRA (Lv24)
CARD NUMBER: 064
RARITY: Uncommon
NOTES: Pokémon Power: Once each turn trash one card from hand and draw one from deck.

"BAD" ALAKAZAM (Lv30)
CARD NUMBER: 065
RARITY: Holofoil
NOTES: First attack: After attacking opponent, can trade with your benched Pokémon.

MACHOP (Lv24)
CARD NUMBER: 066
RARITY: Common

"BAD" MACHOKE (Lv28)
CARD NUMBER: 067
RARITY: Uncommon
NOTES: Attack swaps opponents active Pokémon with benched. First you choose for 20, second they choose.

"BAD" MACHAMP (Lv30)
CARD NUMBER: 068
RARITY: Holofoil
NOTES: Second attack: Make opponent remove active Pokémon and shuffle back into deck.

PONYTA (Lv15)
CARD NUMBER: 077
RARITY: Common

"BAD" RAPIDASH (Lv24)
CARD NUMBER: 078
RARITY: Common
NOTES: Second attack: You can remove one Fire Energy and cause 10 damage to any visible opponent Pokémon.

SLOWPOKE (Lv16)
CARD NUMBER: 079
RARITY: Common
NOTES: First attack: Pull energy card from deck and attach to this Pokémon, then shuffle.

"BAD" SLOWBRO (Lv27)
CARD NUMBER: 080
RARITY: Holofoil
NOTES: Pokémon Power: Once when made active, can search trash pile for three Pokémon or Evolution cards.

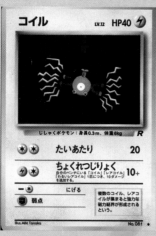

MAGNEMITE (Lv12)
CARD NUMBER: 081
RARITY: Common
NOTES: Second attack: 10 extra damage done for each Magnemite/Magneton/Bad Magneton on bench.

"BAD" MAGNETON (Lv26)
CARD NUMBER: 082
RARITY: Holofoil
NOTES: Second attack: Can remove Energy card from opponent's active and place on any benched Pokémon.

GRIMER (Lv10)
CARD NUMBER: 088
RARITY: Common

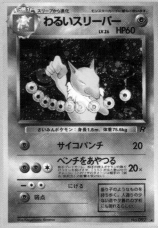

"BAD" MUK (Lv25)
CARD NUMBER: 089
RARITY: Uncommon
NOTES: Pokémon Power: When active, opponent must discard two additional cards to retreat.

DROWZEE (Lv10)
CARD NUMBER: 096
RARITY: Common
NOTES: Pokémon Power: Flip coin, if heads opponent sleeps, if tails you sleep.

"BAD" HYPNO (Lv26)
CARD NUMBER: 097
RARITY: Holofoil
NOTES: Second attack: Opponent throws coin for each benched Pokémon, damage is 20x number of tails.

VOLTORB (Lv13)
CARD NUMBER: 100
RARITY: Common

"BAD" ELECTRODE (Lv24)
CARD NUMBER: 101
RARITY: Uncommon
NOTES: Second attack: Remove all Energy cards and attach to any benched Pokémon.

KOFFING (Lv12)
CARD NUMBER: 109
RARITY: Common

Pokémon TCG Fossil Expansion Player's Guide

"BAD" WEEZING (Lv24)
CARD NUMBER: 110
RARITY: Holofoil
NOTES: First attack causes 20x number of Weezing, Koffing or Bad Weezing on both benches, plus 20 to those.

MAGIKARP (Lv06)
CARD NUMBER: 129
RARITY: Common
NOTES: Second attack: Choose a card that evolves from Magikarp from deck, then shuffle.

"BAD" GYARADOS (Lv31)
CARD NUMBER: 130
RARITY: Holofoil
NOTES: Pokémon Power: When knocked out, opponent takes 20x number of Water cards on Gyarados.

EEVEE (Lv09)
CARD NUMBER: 133
RARITY: Common
NOTES: Second attack causes opponent to flip coin next turn, if tails, their attack fails.

"BAD" VAPOREON (Lv28)
CARD NUMBER: 134
RARITY: Uncommon
NOTES: Second attack causes opponent to remove one energy card.

"BAD" JOLTEON (Lv23)
CARD NUMBER: 135
RARITY: Uncommon
NOTES: Second attack causes opponent to flip coin, if heads then paralyzed, if tails then Jolteon gets 10 damage.

"BAD" FLAREON (Lv23)
CARD NUMBER: 136
RARITY: Uncommon
NOTES: Second attack causes 30+20 more if heads flipped. Must trash a fire energy card.

PORYGON (Lv20)
CARD NUMBER: 137
RARITY: Common
NOTES: First attack can change opponent's Pokémon's weakness to any color except colorless.

DRATINI (Lv12)
CARD NUMBER: 147
RARITY: Common
NOTES: Flip a coin, if heads then opponent is paralyzed.

"BAD" DRAGONAIR (Lv28)
CARD NUMBER: 148
RARITY: Uncommon
NOTES: Pokémon Power lets you select an evolution card from deck to show opponent and put in hand.

"BAD" DRAGONITE (Lv33)
CARD NUMBER: 149
RARITY: Holofoil
NOTES: Pokémon Power lets you choose two basic Pokémon from deck to put in hand. Can use only once.

TRAINER: CHALLENGE!
(or "HITMONLEE'S FOOT")
RARITY: Uncommon
NOTES: Both player's take as many basic Pokémon cards from deck as they want, then shuffle decks.

TRAINER: IMPOSTER PROF. OAK'S ATTACK
RARITY: Uncommon
NOTES: Opponent must trash hand and choose four new cards from deck. You must discard one card.

TRAINER: POKÉMON POWER FUMIGATION
RARITY: Common
NOTES: Until end of opponent's next turn, no Pokémon Powers can be used.

TRAINER: HERE COMES THE ROCKETS!
RARITY: Super-Rare Card!
NOTES: One of the rarest cards available (keep it!). Both players turn side cards face up for rest of game.

TRAINER: GARBAGE COLLECTION
RARITY: Common
NOTES: Choose up to three Pokémon, Evolution or Energy cards from discard pile to put in hand. Shuffle.

TRAINER: SLEEP! SLEEP!
RARITY: Common
NOTES: Flip coin, if heads, opponent's Pokémon sleeps.

TRAINER: TEAM ROCKET'S LITTLE SISTER
RARITY: Holofoil
NOTES: View opponent's hand and pick one Trainer to shuffle back into their deck.

TRAINER: THE BOSS'S WAY/GIOVANNI
RARITY: Uncommon
NOTES: Select one "Bad" Pokémon from deck to show and put in hand, then shuffle.

TRAINER: HOLES ON BATTLEFIELD: Common
NOTES: Each player takes turns flipping, starting with you. First tails causes 10 damage to active Pokémon.

ENERGY: FULL HEAL ENERGY
RARITY: Common
NOTES: Use as a colorless Energy card. Remove one damage counter to Pokémon when attaching.

ENERGY: RAINBOW ENERGY
RARITY: Holofoil
NOTES: Can use as any color energy card, but causes 10 damage to Pokémon it gets attached to.

ENERGY: POTION ENERGY
RARITY: Common
NOTES: Use as a colorless Energy card. Heals Pokémon it's attached to of poison, sleep, confusion, paralyzed.

"GYM LEADERS EXPANSION"

Starting in 1998, Media Factory began producing what are known as the "Gym Leader" sets of Pocket Monster Card Game cards. With these sets, they introduced some interesting new concepts and mechanics into the card game. Each Gym Leaders monster card has a "Trainer" associated with the Pokémon, and a new class of cards ("Stadium" cards) were introduced. Apparently the game was ready for a minor set of new rules to spice up the environment.

Each Pokémon from the Gym Leaders card sets are slightly more powerful than previously released cards. In many cases it takes a little less energy to power a slightly more powerful attack than the same monsters found in earlier sets. Game balance is maintained however with an added restriction: ownership. Every Gym Leaders Pokémon card has a popular Trainer listed next to the monster's name and their face is pictured in the lower right corner of the card. These Trainer's Pokémon will only evolve from Basic Pokémon owned by the same Trainer. For example, Brock's Sandslash will only evolve from Brock's Sandshrew. However, the same set of core game rules are used with these new cards, and the sets are generally compatible. It may become more challenging to build multi-colored decks with Pokémon from many different Trainers, but multi-colored decks normally take significantly more effort to build correctly anyway.

The Gym Leaders Expansion sets (Gym Expansion #1 and Gym Expansion #2) are very confusing for many people because they try to lump the cards they find in the *theme decks* with cards from the Gym #1 and Gym #2 *expansion sets*. They should *not* lump these together. Altogether there are *eight!* (8) different "Gym" Sets of cards to collect:

If you were collecting japanese cards, you would want to buy *sealed* (unopened) Gym *theme* decks and *not* open them. These *sets* (decks) are *fixed* (you *always* get the *same* cards in them no matter how many different copies of the deck you buy.) Any particular card out of one of these decks is *not* valuable unless it is accompanied by all of the other cards, plus the box, plus the plastic coin, plus the rule books, etc.

What many people are confused about is that some of the cards that can be found in the Theme decks look identical to cards from the two expansion sets *almost!* Most people overlook this *almost* part... *all of the theme deck cards do not have rarity symbols.* So, even if everything else looks exactly the same, you *could not* try to sell a Gym Expansion #1 Set unless *all* of the cards had rarity symbols, and you can *only* find cards with rarity symbols from Gym Expansion booster packs (*not* from the theme decks).

It is different with the U.S. cards (and this is the source of most of the confusion). Wizards of the Coast decided to print rarity symbols on the theme deck cards. These cards are *identical* to unlimited edition booster pack cards in every sense. So if you are collecting your unlimited edition Jungle set, and *only* missing a Kangaskhan Foil card... No need to buy any more booster packs! Just buy the "Power Reserve" theme deck that comes with a Kangaskhan foil card. It will cost $10, but this will be a significantly smaller investment than trying to find this specific holographic card out of random Booster packs.

Brock's Deck

Misty's Deck

Lt. Surge's Deck

Erika's Deck

Sabrina's Deck

Blaine's Deck

NOT PICTURED: Gym Expansion #1, Gym Expansion #2

GYM LEADERS 1

JAPANESE SET COMPOSITION

The "Gym Leaders Expansion" is the fourth expansion set of PMCG cards released via booster packs in Japan. It is designed as a follow-up to the first four Gym Leaders Theme Decks previously released (Brock, Misty, Lt. Surge, and Erika). At the time of this printing, the Gym Leaders Theme Decks and Gym Leaders Expansion does not have an expected North American release date.

96 TOTAL CARDS

AVAILABLE IN:

"Booster" Packs:
- 291 Yen (approximately $4.00 as an import)
- 10 cards
  - 1 Rare (Foil)
  - 1 Rare (non-Foil)
  - 3 Uncommon
  - 5 Common
  - no Basic Energy cards

BY RARITY

- 16 Rare (Foil)
- 16 Rare (non-Foil)
- 32 Uncommon
- 32 Common

NOTE: Some of the cards of this set (but not all of them) are available in fixed 64 card "Gym Leader Theme Decks" which were released prior to this set. Cards that were taken from Theme Decks will be distinguishable by the lack of rarity symbols on them. (Since the "theme" decks are fixed sets, there are no true rarities associated with those cards.)

BY TRAINER

Takeshi (Brock):
- 1 Gym Leader Card
- 1 Stadium Card
- 3 Trainer Cards
- 18 Pokémon Cards:
  - 12 Fighting:
    - 7 Basic Pokémon
    - 4 Stage 1 Evolutions
    - 1 Stage 2 Evolutions
  - 3 Fire:
    - 2 Basic Pokémon
    - 1 Stage 1 Evolutions
  - 2 Grass:
    - 1 Basic Pokémon
    - 1 Stage 1 Evolutions
  - 1 Colorless:
    - 1 Basic Pokémon

Erika (Erika):
- 1 Gym Leader Card
- 1 Stadium Card
- 5 Trainer Cards
- 18 Pokémon Cards:
  - 13 Grass:
    - 8 Basic Pokémon
    - 3 Stage 1 Evolutions
    - 2 Stage 2 Evolutions
  - 5 Colorless:
    - 3 Basic Pokémon
    - 2 Stage 1 Evolutions

Kasumi (Misty):
- 1 Gym Leader Card
- 1 Stadium Card
- 4 Trainer Cards
- 15 Pokémon Cards:
  - 15 Water:
    - 9 Basic Pokémon
    - 6 Stage 1 Evolutions

Mathisu (Lt. Surge):
- 1 Gym Leader Card
- 1 Stadium Card
- 4 Trainer Cards
- 12 Pokémon Cards:
  - 7 Lightning:
    - 5 Basic Pokémon
    - 2 Stage 1 Evolutions
  - 5 Colorless:
    - 3 Basic Pokémon
    - 2 Stage 1 Evolutions

Team Rocket (Team Rocket):
- 5 Stadium Cards
- 1 Trainer Card
- 3 Pokémon Cards:
  - 1 Grass:
    - 1 Basic Pokémon
  - 1 Fire:
    - 1 Basic Pokémon
  - 1 Fighting:
    - 1 Basic Pokémon

Note: *Description* and *Name* will be english equivalents.
This list is sorted to match the Media Factory (Japanese) Card List (trainer, then color, then number)

SANDSHREW (Lv20)
CARD NUMBER: 027
RARITY: Common
NOTES: After attack opponent cannot run away on its next turn, a coin toss of heads gives +10 damage to enemy.

SANDSLASH (Lv34)
CARD NUMBER: 028
RARITY: Uncommon
NOTES: First attack: 20 damage and holds no restraints by the opponent's Pokémon power, weakness, or other effects.

VULPIX (Lv10)
CARD NUMBER: 037
RARITY: Common
NOTES: Second attack: 10 points damage plus additional 20 points damage if you flip heads on a coin toss.

VULPIX (Lv16)
CARD NUMBER: 037
RARITY: Uncommon
NOTES: 20 points damage to active Pokémon, and 10 damage to choice Pokémon on their bench.

NINETALES (Lv30)
CARD NUMBER: 038
RARITY: Holofoil
NOTES: Pokémon Power: Can change into another evolved Pokémon by placing on this card. Change back anytime.

ZUBAT (Lv11)
CARD NUMBER: 041
RARITY: Common
NOTES: Second attack: 10 damage and flip coin, heads poisons opponent.

GOLBAT (Lv 30)
CARD NUMBER: 042
RARITY: Uncommon
NOTES: Second attack: 10 damage (+10 if it's a fighting Pokémon) and 10 damage to all benched Pokémon.

DIGLETT (Lv13)
CARD NUMBER: 050
RARITY: Common
NOTES: Second attack: 40 damage (+10 if it's a fighting Pokémon) and 10 damage to all Pokémon on the field.

MANKEY (Lv12)
CARD NUMBER: 056
RARITY: Common
NOTES: Second attack: 40 damage attack decreases 10 points per damage counter that Mankey has on it.

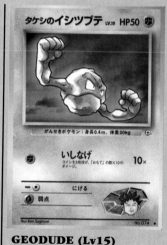

PRIMEAPE (Lv32)
CARD NUMBER: 057
RARITY: Uncommon
NOTES: Pokémon Power: When HP is reduced to 10, can put it and cards attached back in deck and shuffle.

GEODUDE (Lv13)
CARD NUMBER: 074
RARITY: Common
NOTES: Second attack: 30 damage, flip a coin, if heads choose 1 of opponent's Pokémon and add 30 damage.

GEODUDE (Lv15)
CARD NUMBER: 074
RARITY: Common
NOTES: 10 damage and flip a coin 3 times, each heads is 10 damage to opponent.

GRAVELER (Lv32)
CARD NUMBER: 075
RARITY: Uncommon
NOTES: Second attack: 50 damage to both activated Pokémon and 10 damage to every player on both benches.

GOLEM (Lv40)
CARD NUMBER: 076
RARITY: Rare
NOTES: First attack: 20 damage to opponent's Pokémon and 10 damage to up to 3 on their bench.

ONIX (Lv41)
CARD NUMBER: 095
RARITY: Common
NOTES: First attack: Coin toss determines if opponent gets paralyzed.

LICKITUNG (Lv24)
CARD NUMBER: 108
RARITY: Uncommon
NOTES: Second attack: 30 damage plus 2 coin flips to add 20 damage each heads.

RHYHORN (Lv29)
CARD NUMBER: 111
RARITY: Common
NOTES: Flip coin twice if it comes up tails either time this attack fails.

RHYDON (Lv38)
CARD NUMBER: 112
RARITY: Holofoil
NOTES: Pokémon Power: When benched Rhydon can take damage in place of other Pokémon.

POCKET MONSTERS SERIES 5: GYM #1 • BROCK
(continued)

TRAINER

タケシ

自分の場のすべてのポケモンから、それぞれ１つずつダメージカウンターをとりのぞく。

TRAINER: BROCK
RARITY: Rare
NOTES: Take off one damage counter from all your fighting and benched Pokémon.

TRAINER

タケシの育て方

あなたの山札から「タケシのポケモン」（たねポケモンカードまたは 進化カード）を１枚選び出し、相手プレイヤーに見せてから、手札に加える。その後、その山札をよく切る。

BROCK'S ONIX
RARITY: Uncommon
NOTES: Pick a Pokémon from your deck (show it to your opponent) add it to your hand. Reshuffle your deck.

TRAINER

思い出させる

あなたの対戦ポケモンが進化カードなら、この番だけ、進化前に持っていたワザを自分のワザとして使ってよい。

SLOWPOKE'S BRAIN
RARITY: Uncommon
NOTES: If your Pokémon is evolved this card will allow you to use an attack of its primary form once.

TRAINER

タケシの保護

このカードは、あなたの場の「タケシのポケモン」につけて使う。（そのポケモンが場をはなれるまで、このカードはついたまま）
このカードをつけているポケモンのエネルギーカードは、相手の使うワザや、相手の使うトレーナーカードによっては、はがされない。

BROCK'S NUMBER ONE
RARITY: Rare
NOTES: Attaches to any energy card and prevents it from being removed as long as it's on the field of battle.

TRAINER

ニビシティジム   スタジアムカード

このスタジアムカードが場にあるかぎり、「タケシのポケモン」が使うワザのダメージは「抵抗力」の影響を受けない。
このスタジアムカードは、バトル場の横に出して使う。新しいスタジアムカードが場に出た時、古いスタジアムカードはトラッシュされる。

ROCK STADIUM
RARITY: Uncommon
NOTES: When in play all of Brock's cards will not be affected by opponent's persistance. (If another stadium card is played this card is trashed).

PSYDUCK (Lv18)
CARD NUMBER: 054
RARITY: Common
NOTES: Flip coin 3 times. 1 head=take card from deck; 2=20 damage to opponent; 3=use any opponent's power against them.

GOLDUCK (Lv32)
CARD NUMBER: 055
RARITY: Holofoil
NOTES: Flip a coin if heads take away 1 energy card from each of your opponent's Pokémon.

POLIWAG (Lv16)
CARD NUMBER: 060
RARITY: Common
NOTES: Second attack: Pick one of opponent's attacks and the next turn they can't use that attack.

POLIWHIRL (Lv37)
CARD NUMBER: 061
RARITY: Uncommon
NOTES: Second attack: Flip coin for each of water energy cards attached, +10 damage per heads.

TENTACOOL (Lv16)
CARD NUMBER: 072
RARITY: Uncommon
NOTES: Second attack: 20 damage and flip a coin, if heads opponent can't add an energy card to that Pokémon.

TENTACRUEL (Lv30)
CARD NUMBER: 073
RARITY: Holofoil
NOTES: Pokémon Power: You can swap with a benched Pokémon if not affected by sleep, confuse, etc.

POCKET MONSTERS SERIES 5: GYM #1 • MISTY
(continued)

SEEL (Lv14)
CARD NUMBER: 086
RARITY: Common
NOTES: First attack: 10 damage and opponent cannot retreat on his turn.

DEWGONG (Lv40)
CARD NUMBER: 087
RARITY: Uncommon
NOTES: Second attack: 60 point damage to opponent and 20 damage to yourself.

HORSEA (Lv10)
CARD NUMBER: 116
RARITY: Common
NOTES: Second attack: 20 damage and opponent has to flip a coin whether or not their next attack will fail.

HORSEA (Lv16)
CARD NUMBER: 116
RARITY: Common
NOTES: Opponent flips coin each time they attack to see if it works. Lasts as long as their Pokémon is in play.

SEADRA (Lv30)
CARD NUMBER: 117
RARITY: Holofoil
NOTES: Second attack: 30 damage plus 2 coin flips resulting in heads adds 60 damage to opponent.

GOLDEEN (Lv10)
CARD NUMBER: 118
RARITY: Common
NOTES: Second attack: A coin toss of heads leaves your opponent confused.

STARYU (Lv16)
CARD NUMBER: 120
RARITY: Common
NOTES: 20 damage + flip heads to put this card and all cards attached back into hand.

MAGIKARP (Lv05)
CARD NUMBER: 129
RARITY: Common
NOTES: During turn user flips coin, if heads Magikarp can't be hurt on next turn.

GYARADOS (Lv42)
CARD NUMBER: 130
RARITY: Holofoil
NOTES: Pokémon Power: Flip 2 coins, if both are tails Gyarados leaves back to deck.

TRAINER: MISTY
RARITY: Rare
NOTES: Add 20 points damage to an attack. Must discard 2 cards in your hand for this attack to work.

TRAINER:
MISTY'S HEAL
RARITY: Common
NOTES: Discard a card from your hand and take 2 water energy cards from your deck (show opponent), reshuffle.

TRAINER:
MISTY'S PEACE
RARITY: Common
NOTES: 2 players play Rock, paper, scissors game. Winner draws 5 new cards and shuffles old hand into deck.

TRAINER:
MISTY'S ANGER
RARITY: Uncommon
NOTES: Draw 7 cards from your deck, pick 2 and trash the rest.

TRAINER:
MISTY'S LOVE
RARITY: Rare

STADIUM:
WATER STADIUM
RARITY: Uncommon
NOTES: Misty's Pokémon in this Gym will need one less energy card to retreat than the required amount.

POCKET MONSTERS COLLECTOR'S GUIDE

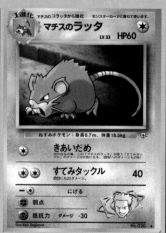

RATTATA (Lv07)
CARD NUMBER: 19
RARITY: Common
NOTES: First attack: By storing up energy Rattata's next attack will be double the damage.

RATICATE (Lv33)
CARD NUMBER: 20
RARITY: Uncommon
NOTES: First attack gives opponent half the damage that opponent already has.

SPEAROW (Lv17)
CARD NUMBER: 21
RARITY: Common
NOTES: First attack: 10 damage and sends opponent's activated Pokémon to bench for another (their choice).

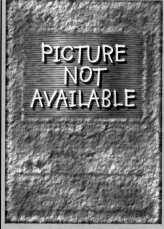

FEAROW (Lv30)
CARD NUMBER: 22
RARITY: Holofoil
NOTES: Second attack: 30 points damage on opponent and on next turn they cannot retreat.

PIKACHU (Lv10)
CARD NUMBER: 25
RARITY: Common
NOTES: 10 damage plus additional 20 if a coin toss results in heads.

MAGNEMITE (Lv10)
CARD NUMBER: 81
RARITY: Common
NOTES: Second attack: 20 damage and flip a coin, heads, opponent is confused.

MAGNEMITE (Lv12)
CARD NUMBER: 081
RARITY: Common
NOTES: First attack: 10 points damage and a coin flip to determine if opponent is paralyzed.

MAGNETON (Lv30)
CARD NUMBER: 082
RARITY: Holofoil
NOTES: Pokémon Power: On field Magneton can draw to it electric cards from your bench.

VOLTORB (Lv12)
CARD NUMBER: 100
RARITY: Common
NOTES: Second attack; hits opponent with 20HP damage. Flip coin heads twice for +20 damage.

ELECTABUZZ (Lv28)
CARD NUMBER: 125
RARITY: Holofoil
NOTES: Second attack: 20 damage that causes you to trash electric card or send it to your benched Pokémon.

JOLTEON (Lv32)
CARD NUMBER: 133
RARITY: Uncommon
NOTES: First attack: choose card from opponent's hand, look at it, give it back to shuffle back into their deck.

EEVEE (Lv10)
CARD NUMBER: 135
RARITY: Rare
NOTES: 30 damage +10 for each damage counter on Jolteon then flip coin, if heads, additional 30 damage.

POCKET MONSTERS COLLECTOR'S GUIDE

TRAINER
マチス

あなたのバトル場にいるポケモン
をベンチにもどし手札から「たね
ポケモン」を直接バトル場に出す。
（あなたのベンチに空きがない時、こ
のカードは使えない）

LT. SURGE
RARITY: Rare
NOTES: Swap a Pokémon from your bench with a Basic Pokémon in your hand. This card cannot be used if there's no room on the bench.

TRAINER
エネルギーサーキュレート

あなたの場のポケモンについてい
る「基本エネルギーカード」を
好きなだけはがし、手札に戻して
よい。

ENERGY VORTEX
RARITY: Common
NOTES: Remove as many energy cards from your benched Pokémon and put it back in your hand.

TRAINER
スパイ作戦

相手プレイヤーの手札を見る。
その後、のぞむなら、あなたの手札
からカードを好きなだけトラッシ
ュして、トラッシュしたのと同じ数
のカードを、山札から引いてよい。

SURVEILLANCE
RARITY: Uncommon
NOTES: Look at opponent's hand, then discard as many of your cards as you wish and draw that equal number from your deck.

TRAINER
マチスの交渉

お互いにサイドカードを1枚ずつ取るかどうか、
相手プレイヤーにたずねる。
オーケーなら、お互いのプレイヤーは、それぞ
れ自分のサイドカードから1枚を選び、取って
手札に加える。
オーケーでないなら、あなたは山札からカード
を1枚引く。

LT. SURGE'S HANDSHAKE
RARITY: Uncommon
NOTES: Both players can take a prize card by consent of the opponent, if not user gets to draw a card from the deck.

TRAINER
マチスの秘策

あなたは、手札からカードを1枚選び、うらにしてベンチ
に出してよい。そのカードは「たねポケモン」でなくても
よく、うらになっている限り、「たねポケモン」としてあ
つかわれる。
のぞむなら、あなたの番の中で、あなたはいつでもそのカ
ードをおもてにしてよい。
そのカードが「ワザ・特殊能力」を使う時や、「進化・にげ
る」をする時、また、そのカードが「ダメージや効果」を
受ける時を持ち、そのカードをおもてにする。
（おもてにしたカードが「たねポケモン」でなかった場合、そのカードと、そ
れについているすべてのカードをトラッシュする）

LT. SURGE'S AIM
RARITY: Rare
NOTES: Can pick 1 card from hand and put face down on bench to use as basic Pokémon.

TRAINER
クチバシティジム   スタジアムカード

お互いのプレイヤーは、のぞむなら、自分の番で「マチ
スのポケモン」がワザを使う番、コインを投げてもよい。
「コインが「おもて」なら、そのワザによって相手の対戦
ポケモンに与えるダメージは「＋10」される。（控えポ
ケモンへのダメージは、そのまま）
「うら」なら、ワザを使ったポケモン自身にも、その
ワザのダメージとして、10ダメージ。
（このスタジアムカードは、バトル場に場に出して使う、別のスタ
ジアムカードが場に出た時、このカードをトラッシュする。）

LASER STADIUM
RARITY: Uncommon
NOTES: Flipping a coin heads results with 10 damage to opponent, tails 10 to user. if agreed to, card can be played per turn.

POCKET MONSTERS SERIES 5: GYM #1 • ERIKA

BULBASAUR (Lv15)
CARD NUMBER: 001
RARITY: Uncommon
NOTES: Flip a coin. If heads pick trainer card out of deck (show it to opponent) put it in your hand and reshuffle.

CLEFAIRY (Lv16)
CARD NUMBER: 035
RARITY: Uncommon
NOTES: First: Flip coin, if heads, pick Pokémon evolved form from deck and place on any of Pokémon, reshuffle.

CLEFABLE (Lv35)
CARD NUMBER: 036
RARITY: Holofoil
NOTES: First attack: Flip a coin, if heads you may take all Pokémon and attached cards on field and put back in hand.

JIGGLYPUFF (Lv13)
CARD NUMBER: 039
RARITY: Common
NOTES: First attack: Remove 1 damage counter on every Pokémon.

ODDISH (Lv10)
CARD NUMBER: 043
RARITY: Common
NOTES: 10 damage and coin toss to see if opponent gets confused (heads) or falls asleep (tails).

ODDISH (Lv15)
CARD NUMBER: 043
RARITY: Common
NOTES: Second attack: 20 damage to opponent and a coin flip of heads to take off 1 damage counter.

GLOOM (Lv24)
CARD NUMBER: 044
RARITY: Uncommon
NOTES: Second attack: Gives 30 damage, drawback is that both opponent and yourself become confused.

VILEPLUME (Lv34)
CARD NUMBER: 045
RARITY: Holofoil
NOTES: Pokémon Power: even if asleep, confused, etc., coin toss is committed to see if opponent gets confused.

PARAS (Lv17)
CARD NUMBER: 046
RARITY: Common
NOTES: Second attack: Flip a coin, if heads opponent becomes poisoned and receives 10 damage on bench.

BELLSPROUT (Lv13)
CARD NUMBER: 069
RARITY: Uncommon
NOTES: Pokémon Power: Once every turn can collect grass energy cards from each of your benched Pokémon.

BELLSPROUT (Lv15)
CARD NUMBER: 069
RARITY: Common
NOTES: 20 damage to your opponent, 10 to yourself.

WEEPINBELL (Lv26)
CARD NUMBER: 070
RARITY: Uncommon
NOTES: Second attack swaps opponent with 1 of their bench Pokémons and attacks it for 20 damage.

VICTREEBEL (Lv37)
CARD NUMBER: 071
RARITY: Rare
NOTES: Pokémon Power: Once per turn you can exchange opponents activated Pokémon with their bench.

EXEGGCUTE (Lv15)
CARD NUMBER: 102
RARITY: Uncommon
NOTES: Second attack: flip a coin, heads = 40 damage, tails = 20 damage to yourself.

EXEGGUTOR (Lv31)
CARD NUMBER: 103
RARITY: Uncommon
NOTES: First attack: Take all cards in your hand, put it back in the deck, shuffle and draw 5 new cards.

TANGELA (Lv21)
CARD NUMBER: 114
RARITY: Common
NOTES: Second attack: Choose opponent's benched Pokémon for 20 damage.

DRATINI (Lv14)
CARD NUMBER: 147
RARITY: Uncommon
NOTES: Pokémon Power: First damage of 20+ on Dratini from basic Pokémon reduced to 10 damage.

DRAGONAIR (Lv32)
CARD NUMBER: 148
RARITY: Holofoil
NOTES: Second attack: Return both active Pokémon and cards attached to deck and shuffle.

TRAINER
エリカ

あなたと相手プレイヤーは、それ
ぞれ、のぞむなら最大3枚まで、
山札からカードを引いてよい。

(あなたがカードを引き終わってから、
相手プレイヤーが引く)

TRAINER: ERIKA
RARITY: Rare
NOTES: If opposing player agrees you both draw 3 cards from your decks (user draws first).

PICTURE NOT AVAILABLE

TRAINER: THINKING
RARITY: Rare

TRAINER
エリカの香水

相手プレイヤーの手札を見る。相
手のベンチに空きがあれば、相手
の手札から「たねポケモン」を好
きなだけ選び、相手のベンチに出
させてよい。

ERIKA'S PERFUME
RARITY: Uncommon
NOTES: Look at the opponentss hand and if there's any Basic Pokémon they must put them down.

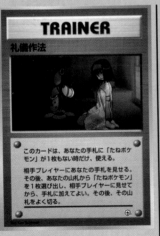

TRAINER
礼儀作法

このカードは、あなたの手札に「たねポケ
モン」が1枚もない時だけ、使える。

相手プレイヤーにあなたの手札を見せる。
その後、あなたの山札から「たねポケモン」
を1枚選び出し、相手プレイヤーに見せて
から、手札に加えてよい。その後、その山
札をよく切る。

KNEELING
RARITY: Uncommon

TRAINER
エリカのお付き

手札からカードを2枚選んで、山札にもど
す。それができない時、このカードは使え
ない。

あなたの山札から「エリカのポケモン」を
最大2枚選び出し、相手プレイヤーに見せ
てから、手札に加えてよい。その後、その
山札をよく切る。

ERIKA'S SERVANTS
RARITY: Uncommon
NOTES: Pick 2 of Erica's Pokémon from deck. (Show to opponent) Take 2 cards from your hand and shuffle them back into the deck.

TRAINER
エリカの親切

お互いの場にいるポケモン全員か
ら、それぞれ、ダメージカウンタ
ーを2つずつとりのぞく。

ERIKA'S UMBRELLA
RARITY: Rare
NOTES: Both players can remove 2 damage counters from their Pokémon.

POCKET MONSTERS SERIES 5: GYM #1 • ERIKA
(continued)

GARDEN STADIUM
RARITY: Uncommon
NOTES: If both players agree each player during their turn may discard an energy card to take 1 damage counter off of a Pokémon.

ROCKET'S HITMONCHAN (Lv29)
CARD NUMBER: 107
RARITY: Holofoil
NOTES: First: On opponent's turnthey must flip coin to determine if they received x2 damage of initial attack.

ROCKET'S SCYTHER (Lv23)
CARD NUMBER: 123
RARITY: Holofoil
NOTES: First: enemy flips coin, if tails Scyther doesn't take damage. Opponent must flip heads to be able to attack scyther again.

ROCKET'S MOLTRES (Lv 26)
CARD NUMBER: 146
RARITY: Holofoil
NOTES: Pokémon Power: (Phoenix) Moltres comes back to life each time K.O.'d. Beat him while asleep, confused, etc.

TRAINER: THAT WAY
RARITY: Holofoil
NOTES: You pick 3 of opponent's cards (without looking). They must take those cards and shuffle them back into their deck.

VERY SMALL STADIUM
RARITY: Common
NOTES: This stadium only allows 4 Pokémon to be used on bench, so when activated any Pokémon over must be returned back to hand.

PRISON STADIUM
RARITY: Rare
NOTES: Both players must discard an extra energy card if they try to retreat a Pokémon.

PSYCHEDELIC STADIUM
RARITY: Rare

FLARE STADIUM
RARITY: Rare
NOTES: If a trainer card is played in this room a coin toss determines who gets to use it. If opponent gets the card they must meet the requirements for using the card, and cannot use it on a card that is attached to a Pokémon. If card is discarded, it is thrown into presenters trash.

NO ENERGY REMOVAL STADIUM
RARITY: Rare
NOTES: In this stadium if either wants to use "Removal" or "Super energy removal" cards they must discard 2 of their cards before doing so.

GYM LEADERS 2

JAPANESE SET COMPOSITION

The "Gym Leaders Expansion #2" is the fifth expansion set of PMCG cards released via booster packs in Japan. It is designed as a follow-up to the fifth and sixth Gym leaders Theme Decks previously released (Blaine and Sabrina). At the time of this printing, the Gym Leaders Theme Decks and Gym Leaders Expansion sets do not have an expected North American release date.

98 TOTAL CARDS

AVAILABLE IN:

"Booster" Packs:
- 291 Yen (approximately $4.00 as an import)
- 10 cards
  - 1 Rare (Foil)
  - 1 Rare (non-Foil)
  - 3 Uncommon
  - 5 Common
  - no Basic Energy cards

BY RARITY	
1	"Super Rare" (non-foil w/white star)
1	"Super Uncommon" (non-foil w/ white diamond)
16	Rare (Foil)
16	Rare (non-Foil)
32	Uncommon
32	Common

NOTE: Some of the cards of this set (but not all of them) are available in fixed 64 card "Gym Leader Theme Decks" which were released prior to this set. Cards that were taken from Theme Decks will be distinguishable by the lack of rarity symbols on them. (Since the "theme" decks are fixed sets, there are no true rarities associated with those cards.)

BY TRAINER

Imakuni? (Imakuni?):
1 Pokémon Card:
  1 Colorless:
    1 Basic Pokémon

_____ (your name here):
1 Pokémon Card:
  1 Colorless:
    1 Basic Pokémon

Takeshi (Brock):
1 Pokémon Card:
  1 Fighting:
    1 Stage 1 Evolution

Kasumi (Misty):
1 Pokémon Card:
  1 Water:
    1 Stage 2 Evolution

Machisu (Lt. Surge):
1 Pokémon Card:
  1 Lightning:
    1 Stage 1 Evolution

Erika (Erika):
2 Pokémon Cards:
  2 Grass:
    1 Stage 1 Evolution
    1 Stage 2 Evolution

Katsura (Blaine):
1 Gym Leader Card
1 Stadium Card
3 Trainer Cards
16 Pokémon Cards:
  11 Fire:
    6 Basic Pokémon
    4 Stage 1 Evolutions
    1 Stage 2 Evolution
  2 Fighting:
    2 Basic Pokémon
  3 Colorless:
    3 Basic Pokémon

Natsumi (Sabrina):
1 Gym Leader Card
1 Stadium Card
3 Trainer Cards
17 Pokémon Cards:
  12 Psychic:
    6 Basic Pokémon
    4 Stage 1 Evolutions
    2 Stage 2 Evolutions
  2 Water:
    1 Basic Pokémon
    1 Stage 1 Evolution
  2 Grass:
    1 Basic Pokémon
    1 Stage 2 Evolution
  1 Colorless:
    1 Basic Pokémon

Kyuo (Koga):
1 Gym Leader Card
1 Stadium Card
3 Trainer Cards
17 Pokémon Cards:
  13 Grass:
    7 Basic Pokémon
    5 Stage 1 Evolutions
    1 Stage 2 Evolution
  4 Colorless:
    3 Basic Pokémon
    1 Stage 1 Evolution

Sakaki (Giovanni):
1 Gym Leader Card
1 Stadium Cards
2 Trainer Cards
15 Pokémon Cards:
  1 Grass:
    1 Basic Pokémon
  1 Fire:
    1 Basic Pokémon
  1 Fighting:
    1 Basic Pokémon

Note: *Description* and *Name* will be english equivalents.
This list is sorted to match the Media Factory (Japanese) Card List (trainer, then color, then number)

ERIKA'S IVYSAUR
CARD NUMBER: 002
RARITY: Uncommon
NOTES: Pokémon Power: If Erica's Ivysaur is on the field all attacks against all Pokémon will be halved.

ERIKA'S VENUSAUR
CARD NUMBER: 003
RARITY: Holofoil
NOTES: Second attack: 20 damage to opponent + 20 damage to 2 of choice Pokémon on the bench.

LT. SURGE'S RAICHU
CARD NUMBER: 026
RARITY: Holofoil
NOTES: 40 damage and coin flip, if heads makes opponent paralyzed, tails and Raichu gets 20 damage.

BROCK'S DUGTRIO
CARD NUMBER: 051
RARITY: Rare
NOTES: Second attack: Dugtrio hides underground and then causes 60 damage to opponent.

MISTY'S POLIWRATH
CARD NUMBER: 062
RARITY: Rare
NOTES: Second attack: Gives both player's benches 10 damage points per Pokémon.

IMAKUNI'S DODUO
CARD NUMBER: 084
RARITY: Common
NOTES: 30 damage to opposing player, but you must sing during your entire attack.

POCKET MONSTERS SERIES 6: GYM #2 • MISCELLANEOUS
(continued)

_____'S CHANSEY
CARD NUMBER: 113
RARITY: Super Rare Card
NOTES: First attack: Flip a coin, if heads Chansey draws 2 cards, if tails, shuffle 2 cards into deck.

POCKET MONSTERS SERIES 6: GYM #2 • BLAINE

CHARMANDER (Lv16)
CARD NUMBER: 004
RARITY: Common
NOTES: First attack: both activated players must discard an energy card.

CHARMELEON (Lv29)
CARD NUMBER: 005
RARITY: Uncommon
NOTES: Second attack: Flip coin for each energy card attached. Each heads gives all opponent's 10 damage.

CHARIZARD (Lv50)
CARD NUMBER: 006
RARITY: Holofoil
NOTES: Regardless of their resistance, a heads toss results in 40 point damage to the opponent.

VULPIX (Lv09)
CARD NUMBER: 037
RARITY: Common
NOTES: Pokémon Power: remove 1 damage counter each turn, if not affected by sleep, confusion, etc.

NINETALES (Lv27)
CARD NUMBER: 038
RARITY: Rare
NOTES: Pokémon Power: Each time that you add an energy card you can take off a damage counter.

MANKEY (Lv14)
CARD NUMBER: 056
RARITY: Common
NOTES: First attack: Flip a coin, if heads pick a card from opponent's discard pile and place it on top of his deck.

GROWLITHE (Lv15)
CARD NUMBER: 058
RARITY: Common
NOTES: Second attack: 20 damage to opponent 10 damage to all of opponent's grass Pokémon.

ARCANINE (Lv42)
CARD NUMBER: 059
RARITY: Holofoil
NOTES: Second attack: Discard 3 fire cards to inflict 120 points of damage on enemy.

PONYTA (Lv13)
CARD NUMBER: 077
RARITY: Common
NOTES: Kicks an opponent for 30 damage and a heads coin toss lets Ponyta run away.

RAPIDASH (Lv31)
CARD NUMBER: 078
RARITY: Uncommon
NOTES: Second attack: 30 damage + flip coin, if heads 10-point damage on opponent's benched Pokémon.

DODUO (Lv17)
CARD NUMBER: 084
RARITY: Common
NOTES: Second attack: Hits opponent with 10 points damage +10 per damage counter on Doduo.

RHYHORN (Lv26)
CARD NUMBER: 111
RARITY: Common
NOTES: Second attack: Gives opponent and their choice of benched Pokémon 20 damage.

KANGASKHAN (Lv36)
CARD NUMBER: 115
RARITY: Uncommon
NOTES: Second attack: 30 damage, +10 damage with a coin flip of heads.

MAGMAR (Lv29)
CARD NUMBER: 126
RARITY: Uncommon
NOTES: Second attack: 20 damage then draw 5 from top of deck, for each fire energy card add another 20 damage.

TAUROS (Lv34)
CARD NUMBER: 128
RARITY: Common
NOTES: Second attack: Flip a coin, each heads = 20 damage to opponent, each tails flip = 20 damage to self.

カツラの ファイヤー LV.44 HP90

かえポケモン：身長2m、体重60kg

ひのとり　90

にげる

弱点

抵抗力　ダメージ -30

No. 146

MOLTRES (Lv44)
CARD NUMBER: 146
RARITY: Holofoil
NOTES: Moltres scorches it's opponent with 90 points of damage then retreats to deck with all cards attached.

TRAINER

カツラ

あなたが「炎」エネルギーカードを手札から出して「カツラのポケモン」につける時、つける「炎」エネルギーカードの枚数を、この番だけ、1枚でなく2枚にする。

TRAINER: BLAINE
RARITY: Rare
NOTES: You may attach 2 Energy cards instead of 1 during this turn.

TRAINER

カツラのギャンブル

あなたの手札から、好きなだけカードを選んでトラッシュする。その後、コインを投げて「おもて」なら、トラッシュした数×2枚のカードを、山札から引いて手札に加える。

BLAINE'S DICE
RARITY: Common
NOTES: Discard any amount of cards from your hand you choose, flip a coin, if heads you draw twice as much cards in which you put down.

TRAINER

カツラの奥の手

このカードは、あなたの手札に「カツラの奥の手」以外のカードがある時には、使えない。
山札からカードを5枚引いて、手札に加える。

BLAINE'S POKE BALL
RARITY: Uncommon
NOTES: Draw 3 cards from the top of your deck. Keep any fire energy cards, the rest you must trash.

TRAINER

カツラのクイズ　その3

あなたの手札から「ポケモン」のカードを1枚選び、おもてを下にして、置く。そのカードが持っているワザの名前を1つ、相手プレイヤーに伝え、そのカードの名前を答えてもらう。

その後、置いたカードをおもてにして、正解なら、相手プレイヤーは山札からカードを3枚引く。不正解でないなら、あなたは山札からカードを3枚引く。

〔置いたカードは、手札にもどす〕

BLAINE'S STARE
RARITY: Uncommon
NOTES: Put a Pokémon card face down. Tell opponent one of its powers. Right guess=he draws 3 cards from his deck, wrong=draw 3 from yours.

TRAINER

グレンタウンジム　　スタジアムカード

お互いのプレイヤーの「カツラのポケモン」は、「水」ポケモンからダメージを受ける時、「弱点」の影響を受けない。

（このスタジアムカードは、バトル場の横に出して使う。このカード以外のスタジアムカードが場に出た時、このカードをトラッシュする）

STADIUM: GUREN TOWN GYM
RARITY: Uncommon
NOTES: In this stadium water attacks will not work on Blaine's Pokémon.

VENONAT (Lv13)
CARD NUMBER: 048
RARITY: Common
NOTES: Second attack: Give opponent 20 damage, flip a coin, if heads discard 1 energy card from opponent.

VENOMOTH (Lv24)
CARD NUMBER: 049
RARITY: Rare
NOTES: First attack: Flip a coin x3, each heads removes one damage counter from all your Pokémon.

PSYDUCK (Lv16)
CARD NUMBER: 054
RARITY: Common
NOTES: Second attack: Give 20 damage to opponent, flip a coin, if heads opponent gets confused, if tails Psyduck is.

GOLDUCK (Lv33)
CARD NUMBER: 055
RARITY: Rare
NOTES: First attack: Remove 10 points damage on your Pokémon and instill them upon opposing Pokémon.

ABRA (Lv11)
CARD NUMBER: 063
RARITY: Common
NOTES: Grab 1 super energy card attached to Abra and put it back into your hand.

KADABRA (Lv41)
CARD NUMBER: 064
RARITY: Uncommon
NOTES: First attack: Flip a coin if heads it all but K.O.s the opponent by leaving them with 10 HP left.

ALAKAZAM (Lv44)
CARD NUMBER: 065
RARITY: Holofoil
NOTES: Pokémon Power: Has the powers a Super Pokémon would have when in play.

SLOWPOKE (Lv15)
CARD NUMBER: 079
RARITY: Common
NOTES: 30 damage and puts opponent to sleep.

SLOWBRO (Lv29)
CARD NUMBER: 080
RARITY: Uncommon
NOTES: First attack: Flip heads and Slowbro goes to sleep reducing its damage by 3 counters.

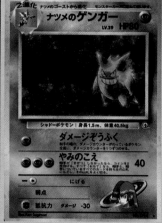

GASTLY (Lv10)
CARD NUMBER: 092
RARITY: Uncommon
NOTES: Pokémon Power: Gastly's HP increases by 10 per Super Energy card that is attached to the card.

HAUNTER (Lv20)
CARD NUMBER: 093
RARITY: Uncommon
NOTES: Flip coin number of Gastlys, Haunters, and Gengars on your field. Every heads gives opponent +30 damage.

GENGAR (Lv39)
CARD NUMBER: 094
RARITY: Holofoil
NOTES: Second attack: If opponent isn't K.O'd by attack, flip coin twice, double heads sends opponent into deck.

POCKET MONSTERS SERIES 5: GYM #2 • SABRINA
(continued)

DROWZEE (Lv15)
CARD NUMBER: 096
RARITY: Common
NOTES: Flip a coin if it is heads the opposing player is hypnotized and cannot attack on next turn.

HYPNO (Lv31)
CARD NUMBER: 097
RARITY: Uncommon
NOTES: First attack: From opponent's trash bring back one basic Pokémon to bench with half its HP.

MR. MIME (Lv20)
CARD NUMBER: 122
RARITY: Common
NOTES: First attack: Swap 3 cards in your hand for 3 energy cards in the deck, reshuffle cards.

JYNX (Lv21)
CARD NUMBER: 124
RARITY: Uncommon
NOTES: First attack: Take off damage counters from an opposing Pokémon, draw cards to number of counters.

PORYGON (Lv17)
CARD NUMBER: 137
RARITY: Common

TRAINER: SABRINA
RARITY: Rare
NOTES: Swap energy cards attached to one of Sabrina's Pokémon with another Pokémon of her gym.

SABRINA'S POKE BALL
RARITY: Common
NOTES: Players count number of cards in their hands, put back in decks, shuffle and draw amount of cards that was in their hand.

SABRINA'S WRATH
RARITY: Uncommon
NOTES: Select a card from opponents discard pile to use for a turn (there are several special requirements).

SABRINA'S ESP
RARITY: Uncommon
NOTES: This card is played attached to a Pokémon for a turn. It gives a Pokémon an extra coin toss for additional damage to an opponent.

STADIUM: YAMABUKI CITY GYM
RARITY: Uncommon
NOTES: During their turn any Sabrina Pokémon can transfer Energy cards unto another Pokémon of choice.

WEEDLE (Lv13)
CARD NUMBER: 013
RARITY: Common
NOTES: Second attack: 10 damage plus a coin flip, heads to poison an opponent, tails to paralyze them.

KAKUNA (Lv21)
CARD NUMBER: 014
RARITY: Uncommon
NOTES: Pokémon Power: Flip a coin if heads a Kakuna evolves. Reshuffle the deck.

BEEDRILL (Lv34)
CARD NUMBER: 015
RARITY: Holofoil
NOTES: Second attack: Flip coin, if heads 70-point damage to opponent, tails misses and attack can't be used again.

PIDGEY (Lv9)
CARD NUMBER: 016
RARITY: Uncommon
NOTES: First attack: Return active Pokémon to deck with all attached Replace with bench, pick Pokémon from deck.

PIDGEY (Lv15)
CARD NUMBER: 016
RARITY: Common
NOTES: 20 damage and a coin toss, if its tails you forfeit Pidgey's next turn.

PIDGEOTTO (Lv34)
CARD NUMBER: 017
RARITY: Rare
NOTES: 10 damage and coin toss of heads adds 30 damage more and Pidgeoto can't be hit on next turn.

EKANS (Lv17)
CARD NUMBER: 023
RARITY: Common
NOTES: Snake bite of 10 damage points, flip a coin twice, if both heads opponent becomes both paralyzed and confused.

ARBOK (Lv44)
CARD NUMBER: 024
RARITY: Rare
NOTES: Second attack: Damage 20 if Arbok is poisoned it's more poisonous, his attack becomes 40 points and opponent is poisoned.

ZUBAT (Lv14)
CARD NUMBER: 041
RARITY: Common
NOTES: +10 damage to opponent for every zubat in play. You can pick as many Blaine Zubats from the deck and play it in your hand.

GOLBAT (Lv27)
CARD NUMBER: 042
RARITY: Uncommon
NOTES: Second attack: 30 damage plus a coin toss to determine if opponent is confused.

GRIMER (Lv19)
CARD NUMBER: 088
RARITY: Common
NOTES: Second attack: Throws sludge for 20 damage.

MUK (Lv38)
CARD NUMBER: 089
RARITY: Rare
NOTES: Pokémon Power: On his turn Muk can use his power to take 1 energy card from opponent and trash it.

KOFFING (Lv10)
CARD NUMBER: 109
RARITY: Common
NOTES: 10 damage to opponent and all surrounding Pokémon.

KOFFING (Lv15)
CARD NUMBER: 109
RARITY: Uncommon
NOTES: Second attack: 30 points damage and flip a coin, if heads Koffing and all attached go back into deck.

WEEZING (Lv31)
CARD NUMBER: 110
RARITY: Uncommon
NOTES: Second attack: A poison gas attack for 20 damage points.

TANGELA (Lv16)
CARD NUMBER: 114
RARITY: Common
NOTES: Second attack: Flip a coin, if heads user draws 2 cards from the deck.

DITTO (Lv12)
CARD NUMBER: 132
RARITY: Holofoil
NOTES: First attack: Ditto can double in size, also doubling his HP total to 80.

TRAINER: KOGA
RARITY: Rare
NOTES: When played, if Koga is harmed during the next turn the opponent is poisoned.

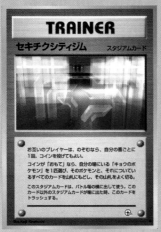

CRYSTAL STADIUM
RARITY: Uncommon

FLYING GARBAGE
RARITY: Common
NOTES: Count the cards in your hand, discard, shuffle them back into your deck and trash the number of cards discarded.

CONTRACT
RARITY: Uncommon
NOTES: You use this card to connect two Pokémon. Whenever you like you can swap between this bench and an activated Pokémon.

The symbol on this Gym #2 Trainer card is nothing to worry about. According to www.zenguide.com this symbol is not a Nazi swastika but a fylfot. "A widely used symbol is the Western Chivalry heraldry design way before Hitler came to power. He actually saw that symbol from a church where he was the altar boy and picked it up, tilted 45 degrees and reversed it to create the Nazi's symbol. In eastern culture, the symbol represent Buddhism just as a cross symbolizes Christianity. It is believed that the Buddha was born with this symbol on his chest. It's a shame that it was twisted and distorted in the last 50 years or so."

NIDORAN (F) (Lv11)
CARD NUMBER: 029
RARITY: Common
NOTES: Second attack: Gives 30 points damage to opponent and 20 to itself.

NIDORINA (Lv35)
CARD NUMBER: 030
RARITY: Uncommon
NOTES: Second attack: 20 points damage and a coin toss to see whether opponent becomes paralyzed.

NIDOQUEEN (Lv51)
CARD NUMBER: 031
RARITY: Rare
NOTES: Second attack: 50 points damage if you flip a heads, 100 points damage if Nidoking is on the bench.

NIDORAN (M) (Lv14)
CARD NUMBER: 032
RARITY: Common
NOTES: Second attack: 20 points damage, but if Nidoran has +20 damage his blow increases 10 points.

NIDORINO (Lv32)
CARD NUMBER: 033
RARITY: Uncommon
NOTES: 20 damage initially, +20 if opponent already is injured.

NIDOKING (Lv58)
CARD NUMBER: 034
RARITY: Holofoil
NOTES: First: Any opposing Pokémon on field with max. HP less than 50 can't attack until Nidoking leaves.

MEOWTH (Lv12)
CARD NUMBER: 052
RARITY: Uncommon
NOTES: First attack: Look at top card of opponents deck, if its a trainer card trash it, anything else goes in his hand.

MEOWTH (Lv17)
CARD NUMBER: 052
RARITY: Common

PERSIAN (Lv22)
CARD NUMBER: 053
RARITY: Holofoil
NOTES: Pokémon Power: "Call the Boss", by playing this card user picks a Giovanni card from deck and place it in hand.

MACHOP (Lv18)
CARD NUMBER: 066
RARITY: Common
NOTES: Second attack: 20 damage +20 more per damage counter they have.

MACHOKE (Lv36)
CARD NUMBER: 067
RARITY: Uncommon
NOTES: First attack: 60 damage if you flip heads. If tails then 100 damage to Machoke.

MACHAMP (Lv50)
CARD NUMBER: 068
RARITY: Holofoil
NOTES: Pokémon Power: If knocked out, Machamp can come back with 10 HP for one last try.

PINSIR (Lv27)
CARD NUMBER: 127
RARITY: Rare
NOTES: Second attack: 40 damage to opponent, flip a coin, if tails, Pinsir sustains 20 damage.

MAGIKARP (Lv9)
CARD NUMBER: 129
RARITY: Common
NOTES: First attack: 40 damage one shot, flip a coin, if tails user misses.

GYARADOS (LV40)
CARD NUMBER: 130
RARITY: Holofoil
NOTES: First attack: Flip 2 coins if both are heads a storm inflicts 20 damage to all bench Pokémon.

TRAINER: GIOVANNI
RARITY: Holofoil
NOTES: Choose 1 of Giovanni's Pokémon in play and immediately evolve it when this card is played.

TRAINER: POOL
RARITY: Common

TRAINER: CONTROL
RARITY: Rare

POCKET MONSTERS SERIES 5: GYM #2 • GIOVANNI (continued)

STADIUM: TOKIWA CITY GYM
RARITY: Rare
NOTES: When a Giovanni Pokémon is playing in this stadium, it can take off 2 damage counters each time it evolves..

POCKET MONSTERS SERIES 5: GYM #2 • TEAM ROCKET

ROCKET'S SNORLAX (LV40)
CARD NUMBER: 143
RARITY: Rare
NOTES: Pokémon Power: Damage inflicted on Snorelax when he's sleeping ricochets 20 damage to its attacker.

ROCKET'S ZAPDOS (LV34)
CARD NUMBER: 145
RARITY: Holofoil
NOTES: Second attack: 70 damage, resulting in 10 points damage off itself for each electric energy attached.

ROCKET'S MEWTWO (LV 35)
CARD NUMBER: 150
RARITY: Holofoil
NOTES: First attack: Flip a coin, if heads Mewtwo and opponent activate exchange damage.

ROCKET'S GANG
RARITY: Uncommon
NOTES: Flip 2 coins, if both are heads, swap 1 of their bench players in for the activated player. His original activated player and all cards attached must go back into the deck and be reshuffled.

ROCKET'S POTION
RARITY: Uncommon
NOTES: Flip a coin, if heads you can pick a card from your deck and add it to your hand. If its tails you cannot use a trainer card until next turn.

TOXIC STADIUM
RARITY: Uncommon
NOTES: When card is played opponent must flip a coin. If heads he must put cards face down on field—these cards can't be used until opponent's next turn.

KILLER MAN-HOLE
RARITY: Uncommon

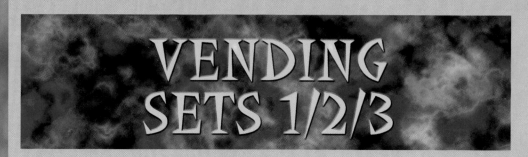

VENDING SETS 1/2/3

Surprise! Surprise! Surprise!
These cards were released in Japan through vending machines on sheets of four cards that peeled off, revealing the Pokémon or various Trainers, Extra Rules, etc.

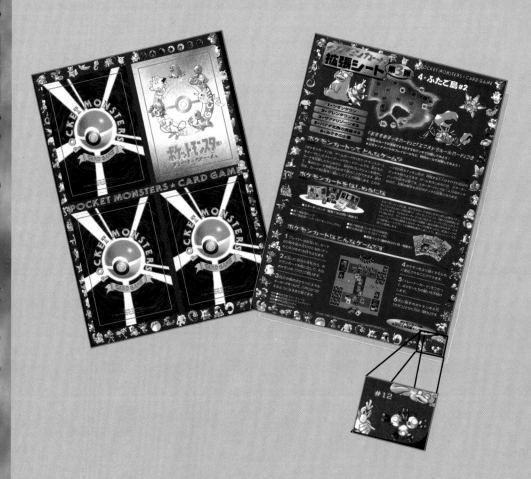

Note: This section is organized with Pokémon in alphabetical order, followed by various other cards.

POCKET MONSTERS VENDING 1/2/3

ABRA
NOTES: Attack: One of opposing players bench Pokémon takes 10 points damage

AERODACTYL

ALAKAZAM

ARBOK
NOTES: Second attack: 30 damage to player and poisons player +10 damage each turn after being poisoned.

ARTICUNO
NOTES: Pokémon Power: When this card is in battle bench cannot be harmed.

BELLSPROUT

BULBASAUR

CATERPIE

CHANSEY

CHARMANDER
NOTES: First attack: After opposing players first attack each of its additional attacks is 10 damage points less.

CLEFAIRY

CUBONE
NOTES: Attack: Flip a coin, If heads opposing player takes 30 damage, if tails their bench gets 10 damage each.

DEWGONG
NOTES: First attack: Take away all damage but must go to sleep.

DITTO

DODRIO
NOTES: Second attack: Flip coin 3 times, each heads gives opposing player 30 points damage.

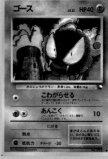

DODUO
NOTES: First attack: After opposing players first attack, each additional attack is 10 damage points less.

EEVEE

ELECTABUZZ

FEAROW

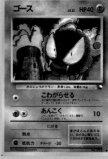

GASTLY
NOTES: Second attack: 10 points damage and opposing player can't use trainer card during their turn.

GENGAR

GEODUDE
NOTES: Second attack: enemy attacks under 20 points of damage will not count.

GOLBAT
NOTES: First attack: the amount of damage that is given to the opponent is taken of off itself.

GOLDUCK

POCKET MONSTERS VENDING 1/2/3
(continued)

GOLEM

GRAVELER (LV 26)
NOTES: Second attack: Earthquake – your benched Pokémon receive 10 damage each, also.

GRAVELER (LV 27)
NOTES: Pummel rock – flip two coins, heads x10 damage goes to opponent's benched Pokémon of your choice.

GRIMER
NOTES: First attack: when opponent retreats Pokémon, requires twice the energy cards.

GROWLITHE
NOTES: First attack: Flip a coin, if heads can pick Trainer card out of deck (show to opponent).

HAUNTER (LV 25)
NOTES: Second attack: Number of opponents used Side Cards x10 damage.

HAUNTER (LV26)
NOTES: First attack: see opponent's hand, then damage of number of Trainer cards x10.

HITMONCHAN
NOTES: Flip a coin, if heads then damage opponent benched Pokémon of choice for 10 damage.

HITMONLEE
NOTES: First attack: flip two coins, number of heads x30 damage.

HORSEA
NOTES: Second Attack: Up to two extra water cards can give up to 20 extra damage to opponent

HYPNO

JYNX
NOTES: Cold Breath: Flip a coin, if heads, then opponent sleeps.

KABUTO

NOTES: Pokémon Power - If you have evolved Pokémon showing, can flip a coin, if heads, take back unevolved cards of Pokémon.

KADABRA (LV 39)

NOTES: First attack: use this attack on psychic Pokémon and they get double damage.

KADABRA (LV 40)

NOTES: Second attack: next turn if opponent adds an energy card they get paralyzed

KAKUNA

NOTES: Pokémon Power-Poison Acid: When opponent attacks, they get poisoned.

KANGASKHAN

NOTES: Second attack: flip two coins, attack only works if both coins tails.

KINGLER

NOTES: Second attack: attacks for 80, but you get double damage on next attack from opponent.

KOFFING

NOTES: Pokémon Power: Can call another Koffing out of deck to put on bench if room (even if poisoned, etc).

KRABBY

NOTES: First attack: flip a coin, if heads then opponent is paralyzed

LAPRAS

NOTES: First attack: Flip a coin, if heads opponent sleeps.

LICKITUNG

NOTES: Second attack: flip a coin, if heads, 10 more damage.

MACHAMP

MACHOKE (LV 24)

NOTES: Second attack: flip a coin, if heads, 20 damage to Pokémon you choose on opponent's bench.

POCKET MONSTERS VENDING 1/2/3
(continued)

MACHOKE (LV 28)
NOTES: Second attack: Flip a coin, if heads, then +20 damage.

MACHOP
NOTES: First attack: Flip coin, if heads, next turn use Head Butt (2nd) for 2x damage. If tails, no damage

MAGMAR
NOTES: First attack: Discard Fire cards from any Pokémon in play for 10x damage.

MAGNEMITE

MAGNETON
NOTES: Pick opponent Pokémon, flip coin, if heads can trash one energy card.

MAROWAK
NOTES:

METAPOD
NOTES: When Pokémon is on bench, grass Pokémon weak points don't count.

MEWTWO (LV 30)

MEWTWO (LV 54)
NOTES: Number of psychic Pokémon on bench x10 damage.

MEWTWO (LV 67)
NOTES: Second attack: 30 points damage and flip a coin if heads discard 1 of opponents energy cards.

MOLTRES
NOTES: First attack: Pick opponent Pokémon. Flip a coin until tails, number of heads before, take off in energy cards.

MR. MIME
NOTES: Pokémon Power - When on bench, both sides Pokémon resistance and weak point don't count.

Pokémon TCG Fossil Expansion Player's Guide   POCKET MONSTERS COLLECTOR'S GUIDE • 141

NIDORAN (F)
NOTES: First attack: Flip a coin, if heads opponent loses a turn.

NIDORAN (M)
NOTES: Second attack: rams the opponent for a second hit if you get heads on a coin toss.

NIDORINA
NOTES: First attack: damage +10 for each friend of Nidorina on bench.

NIDORINO
NOTES: Flip a coin, if tails you get 20 damage and opponent gets none.

OMANYTE (LV 20)

OMANYTE (LV 22)
NOTES: Pokémon Power: If you have evolved Pokémon showing, flip coin, if heads, take Mysterious Fossil from trash.

OMASTAR

ONIX
NOTES: Second attack: flip coin, if heads, opponent can't run away on next move.

PARAS
NOTES: Second attack: can call another Paras from inside your deck to come out to bench, then shuffle.

PARASECT
NOTES: Second attack; heal yourself for 20 damage while causing 20 damage to opponent.

PIDGEOTTO
NOTES: Second attack: flip coin, if heads you can't be hurt next turn

PIDGEY
NOTES: Second attack: Flip a coin, if heads, +20 damage.

PIKACHU (LV 5)
NOTES: Second attack: Flip a coin, if heads, can't get damaged next turn.

PIKACHU (LV 13)
NOTES: First attack: 40 damage with the trashing of an energy card.

PINSIR
NOTES: First attack: flip a coin, if heads, +10 damage to opponent.

POLIWAG
NOTES: Flip coin, if heads, opponent is paralyzed.

POLIWHIRL
NOTES: Second attack: flip a coin, if heads, opponent is paralyzed.

POLIWRATH
NOTES: Second attack: extra energy cards over required 3 causes +10 damage each, limit +20 damage.

PONYTA
NOTES: Second attack: Flip coin, if tails, trash 1 opponent energy card. If none to trash, can't attack

PORYGON
NOTES: Second attack: Can change resistance during battle to any type of energy until retreated.

RAICHU
NOTES: Second attack: Pick a Pokémon, number of water energy cards x10 damage.

RAPIDASH
NOTES: Second attack: opponent chooses to swap active Pokémon with any of their benched.

RATTATA
NOTES: Flip a coin, if heads, next turn opponent can't attack.

RHYDON
NOTES: Pick up top 5 deck cards, take any energy, discard rest.

SANDSHREW
NOTES: Second attack: Weakness and Resistance don't matter for attack.

SANDSLASH
NOTES: First attack: Flip 3 coins, heads x10 damage to both you and opponent.

SCYTHER
NOTES: First attack: Can't use attack during next round (use every other turn).

SEADRA
NOTES: Use extra water energy cards for +10 damage to opponent's benched Pokémon, up to 2.

SEEL
NOTES: First attack: Next opponent attack –10 damage.

SHELLDER
NOTES: Use extra water energy cards for +10 damage to opponent's benched Pokémon, up to 2.

SLOWBRO
NOTES: First attack: puts you and opponent to sleep.

SNORLAX
NOTES: Pokémon Power – When on bench, opponent's Pokémon can't retreat.

SPEAROW
NOTES: Pokémon Power: When on bench, opponent's Pokémon can't retreat.

SQUIRTLE
NOTES: First attack: use 2nd attack on next turn for 3x damage.

STARYU
NOTES: First attack: Use 1st, then during opponent's turn your water weakness doesn't apply.

TANGELA

TAUROS
NOTES: Flip coin, if heads add 10 damage, if tails opponent switches active Pokémon with benched (their choice).

VENOMOTH

VENONAT
NOTES: First attack: flip a coin, if heads, pick enemy attack and they can't use on their next turn.

VOLTORB
NOTES: Second attack: Count Voltorbs on both benches x10 damage.

VULPIX
NOTES: Can switch opponent's active and benched Pokémon before attacking.

WEEDLE

WEEPINBELL
NOTES: First attack: take off all damage counters and remove evolve card to go back to Basic Pokémon.

WEEZING
NOTES: Pokémon Power: Can use each turn – flip coin, if heads, poisoned Pokémon get 20 damage instead of 10.

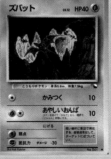

WIGGLYTUFF

ZAPDOS
NOTES: Second attack: If heads, +20 damage, if tails, you get 20 damage.

ZUBAT
NOTES: Second attack: flip coin, if heads, opponent becomes confused

TRAINER: FLASH!
NOTES: Both players take top 5 deck cards and put in any order they want.

POCKET MONSTERS COLLECTOR'S GUIDE

TRAINER
元気のかたまり

BALL OF ENERGY:
NOTES: Trash two energy cards to take one Basic Pokémon from trash.

TRAINER
ポケモンタワー　スタジアムカード

POKÉMON TOWER
NOTES: Both players can't use Trainers or Powers that take cards from trash.

TRAINER
ポケモン再転送

RECYCLE POKÉMON
NOTES: Take evolving Pokémon card from trash, show opponent, and add to hand.

TRAINER
イマクニ？のわるぢえ

IMAKUNI'S BAD IDEA
NOTES: Put this card out, if opponent isn't looking you can remove damage counters, and can deny it when opponent accuses.

TRAINER
マスターボール

MASTER BALL
NOTES: Look at top 7 cards, can take one Basic or evolve card, then shuffle remaining cards back into deck.

TRAINER
月の石

MOON STONE
NOTES: Pick evolution card for colorless Pokémon from deck, show opponent, put in hand, shuffle cards.

TRAINER
化石の発掘

FOSSIL DIG
NOTES: From deck or trash, pick fossil Pokémon for hand. Shuffle decks.

EXTRA RULE
ダグトリオチームバトル 3 vs 3

TEAM BATTLE 3 VS. 3
NOTES: 3 people to 1 team. each brings own deck, play team vs. team. Choose who goes first. Team that wins 2 battles wins match.

EXTRA RULE
「こんらん」で20ダメージルール

CONFUSE 20 DAMAGE
NOTES: If you're confused and try to flip coin, if tails you get 20 damage.

EXTRA RULE
デッキ交換戦

TRADING DECK BATTLE
NOTES: Both people bring deck, battle 3 times. First with own deck, second with opponent's, third with yours. Win with your deck=1 point; their deck=2 points. Most points wins.

EXTRA RULE
3デッキ戦

3 DECK BATTLE
NOTES: Lay out three decks, choose order. Battle three times with decks in order, for best 2 out of 3.

EXTRA RULE
サイドカード4枚戦

4 SIDE CARD BATTLE
NOTES: Battle with four side cards instead of six.

CHECKLIST 1: SECRET OF POKÉMON TOWER
NOTES: (list of cards in deck – basic, evolves, trainers, energy)

CHECKLIST 2: (LOCATION FOR FIRE POKÉMON)
NOTES: (list of cards in deck – basic, evolves, trainers, energy)

CHECKLIST 3: SAFARI ZONE
NOTES: (list of cards in deck – basic, evolves, trainers, energy)

CHECKLIST 4: ISLAND
NOTES: (list of cards in deck – basic, evolves, trainers, energy)

CHECKLIST 5: LAST CAVE
NOTES: (list of cards in deck – basic, evolves, trainers, energy)

IMAKUNI MOLE
NOTES: When you get this card it's a "miss"… not worth anything. "Do you hate "miss" that much?"

IMAKUNI'S COMPUTER
NOTES: Even Imakuni has a computer, and on his day off he goes into his computer to think about the past. (card has no purpose).

IMAKUNI CHATTING
NOTES: "Recently I started Pokémon cards, but there's one thing I wanna say about the cards. You can't even use the Imakuni's cards." (he doesn't think that's fair). "Do you know what Imakuni card does? When you use this card your own Pokémon gets confused." If this card is junk, it's gonna make his fans cry. He has an Imakuni card in his deck, and someday he's going to use it.

CARD FACTORY
NOTES: "This is the location of the secret Pokémon card factory.".

PROMO-MANIA!

The following pages feature "Promotional" cards that have been included as a bonus with various merchandise, mostly in Japan. We've done our best to research the source of each card, and translate any interesting attacks or information they feature. This guide is by no means complete, and there are new cards released all the time in Japan and the US, but we're sure you'll find it interesting.

MAGAZINE PROMOS

This Japanese magazine gives tips on how to become a champion Pocket Monsters player, and included one of the coolest-looking promo cards, for Exeggutor, which included both Japanese and English text.

DIGLET
NOTES: Second attack: Flip a coin to cause 10 hit points more damage.

DUGTRIO
NOTES: Pokémon Power: This card will not be harmed if it is on the bench.

Yet another Japanese guide for Pocket Monster player's, with lots of cute illustrations and these two exclusive trading cards.

PIKACHU RECORDS PROMOS

All Pikachu Records promo cards are marked with a lightning bolt to the bottom-right of the picture. The two packages on this page featured a mini CD (3-inch diameter) with several songs on each. The package on the next page featured a full-sized CD.

MEOWTH'S PARTY

NOTES: When played, user adds all the Pokémon on the playing field and flips a coin to the sum number presented. Each heads initiates 10 hit points damage to the opposing player. While every tail flip instills 10 damage to the user.

Included CD features 5 wacky songs, and there's also a fold out poster with lyrics (in Japanese, of course).

LAPRIS RIDE

Use this card to take 3 damage counters off of any one of its users individual Lapras that is in play. The CD contains four Japanese musical tracks with plenty of high, squeeky voices. There's also a message card inside (left) with a message from the lady that does the voice of Misty in the Japanese animation series.

JAPANESE "POKéMON BEST COLLECTION" CD

The serious Pocket Monster collector will not want to miss out on this great collectible! It's a Japanese music "Pokemon Best Collection" CD packaged with 10 Japanese Promotional cards. The music is nutty and wild, but really fun to listen to! You'll find yourself humming and dancing to the bubbly tunes. Most of us won't have a clue of what the music is all about, but that doesn't matter! This is definitely a keeper for those long, boring car rides when everyone could use a smile and a good laugh. My personal favorite is midway through track #5 when we hear James, Jessie, and Meowth do the "Team Rocket motto" in Japanese. (Although track #6's hip-hop tune is a close second!)

Produced by the "Pikachu Records" label, the packaging is thick and sturdy and comes with a 32 page glossy CD booklet. The booklet details the 13 different songs that are on the compact disc. The face of the CD is adorned with a mosaic of all the most popular Pocket Monsters on a white background. It's too bad that the CD won't fit into a card-binder–It's really something to showcase at serious Pokemon trading sessions. Of course, the CD is a minor treasure compared to the limited print promo cards that are safely housed inside the back cover of the package. The artwork on all of these Promos is unique, but some of these monsters have made prior appearances in the card game. Note that Blastoise, Charizard, and Venusaur have identical game abilities to the U.S. (and Japanese) Base set cards. Their Hit Points, Pokemon Powers, Attack Moves, and other features are all identical. Media Factory retained the same "Level" for these monsters to clearly represent their identical game-play functionality, but in my opinion the art on these promos are ten times more appealing than what you find in the Base set cards.

Beyond those 3 "repeat" Pokemon, 7 all-new cards have been introduced here. Arcanine boasts deck flexibility with an all-colorless attack requirement, and Level 25 Mew has just about the most Hit Points that this popular character will ever see in the card game. The two trainer cards we have identified as "Computer Crash!" and "Super Energy Retrieval" (This one lets you draw FOUR! basic energy cards out of your discard pile for the minor cost of discarding two additional cards from your hand).

Along with these 10 great Japanese cards, the newest copies of this "Best Collection" CD are accompanied by a U.S. Level 12 Pikachu card. It was included as an introduction of the english-version TCG cards to the Japanese Pocket Monster Card Game fans. This Pikachu is identical in every way to non-1st Edition U.S. Base set Pikachu cards, except one: It was printed by Media Factory–not by Wizards of the Coast. Although it uses WOTC's artwork (including all the early revision features–no "shadow" on the picture, "99" in Nintendo's copyright, yellow-cheeked Pikachu), it is printed on the thinner (but more durable) card stock that the Japanese card manufacturer uses. This card will be easy to spot in direct comparison to the U.S. manufac-

tured Pikachu cards, but who knows how many have filtered into the U.S. market and "lost" as common Pikachu cards...This is definitely one of the few instances when a card will fail the "counterfeit" tests, only to prove itself MORE valuable than the original!

MEW (Lv25)
NOTES: Second attack can duplicate opponent's Psychic Attacks.

MEWTWO
NOTES: Second attack: 30 damage to your choice of opponent's Pokémon.

VENUSAUR
NOTES: Pokémon Power: During turn can transfer any of his grass energy to any of your other Pokémon.

BLASTOISE
NOTES: Pokémon Power: During turn may put as many water energy cards on any of your Playing Pokémon.

CHARIZARD
NOTES: Pokémon Power: Any type of energy card becomes a Fire energy card when attached, lasts 1 turn.

ARCANINE
NOTES: Second attack: Discard 2 fire energy cards to attack x10 amount of damage counters on your Pokémon.

COMPUTER RAGE
NOTES: Both players draw 5 cards from their deck to use in their hand.

PORYGON
NOTES: Second attack: Flip a coin x3, 20 damage points for each heads.

SNORLAX

ENERGY EXCHANGE
NOTES: Throw away two cards in hand and take 4 energy cards from discard pile.

Pokémon TCG Fossil Expansion Player's Guide

SOUTHERN ISLANDS PROMOS

The "Southern Islands" card sets were sold in Japan during the theatrical release of the animated short film "Pikachu's Summer Vacation". The set is comprised of 6 different fixed-set packages of 3 cards each. Each package contains 1 holographic card and 2 non-foil cards. The holographic card is slightly unique from previously released holographic cards; instead

of the artwork printed on top of "holographic" foil, the artwork is printed on paper and the card background is instead printed on foil. The six different packages are grouped and labeled as shown on these two pages. Each group of cards also includes an exclusive postcard, and the art on the three cards are small portions of the overall illustration on the postcards.

TOGEPI
NOTES: First attack lets you choose any of opponent's Pokémon for 10 damage, regardless of weak/resist.

LAPRAS
NOTES: First attack— remove two damage counters from you and opponent, and they sleep.

TENTACRUEL
NOTES: First attack lets you flip a coin for each Water attached, then draw 2 cards for each heads.

SQUIRTLE
NOTES: Attack does extra 10 damage for each extra Water attached, up to 20 extra.

KING SLOWPOKE
NOTES: Second attack does extra 10 damage for each energy card on opponent.

AIMED BULLET
NOTES: Choose opponent Pokémon, flip coin for each grass attached to Exeggutor, 10 damage per heads.

Tropical Island: Sea

Tropical Island: Beach

Tropical Island: Jungle

LICKITUNG
NOTES: First attack lets you flip a coin, if heads you can remove 2 damage markers from any Pokémon.

VILEPLUME
NOTES: First attack—flip a coin, if heads, remove 2 damage counters on Vileplume + benched Pokémon.

PRIMEAPE
NOTES: Second attack adds 10 damage for each damage counter on Primeape.

Rainbow Island: Sky

MEW
NOTES: Choose 1 color of Energy attached, all opponent's visible Pokémon of same color take 20 damage.

PIDGEOT
NOTES: First attack requires coin flip, if tails then attack fails.

ONIX
NOTES: FIrst attack does 20 damage for each heads from two flipped coins.

Rainbow Island: Riverside

TOGEPI
NOTES: Attack is Cry Loudly. Flip a coin, if heads, opponent is confused.

IVYSAUR
NOTES: First attack—both players flip coin. If heads, they can remove up to 3 damage counters from any Pokémon.

RATICATE
NOTES: Flip a coin when attacking, if heads opponent takes 30 extra damage.

Rainbow Island: Field of Flowers

LADY-BA
NOTES: Second attack—flip a coin, if heads, opponent's next attack fails.

JIGGLYPUFF
NOTES: First attack lets you swap opponent's active and any benched Pokémon.

BUTTERFREE
NOTES: First attack same as Jigglypuff. Second flips coin for paralyzed (heads) or poison (tails).

ANCIENT EGYPTIAN MEW

The Ancient Egyptian Mew is one of the coolest rare cards available. It's impossible to appreciate the full impact of it from these pictures because the entire background of the card on both sides is a holofoil with very cool colors. The card came well-protected in a thick plastic holder bound inside a large-format movie program (next page). The program also features a catalog of Japanese official Pocket Monsters merchandise (next page, bottom), featuring some very cool items we'd like to find.

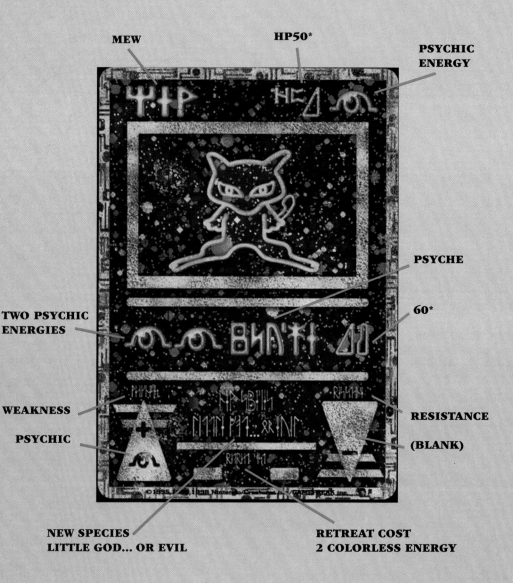

MEW

HP50*

PSYCHIC ENERGY

PSYCHE

TWO PSYCHIC ENERGIES

60*

WEAKNESS

RESISTANCE

PSYCHIC

(BLANK)

NEW SPECIES
LITTLE GOD... OR EVIL

RETREAT COST
2 COLORLESS ENERGY

*A runes translation appeared in a Japanese magazine, with the challenge to translate the entire Ancient Egyptian Mew card for a contest. We did our best to figure things out, but numbers aren't included, so we're guessing the triangle represents 50, and the character after the triangle in the attack strength could possibly represent 10. Either way, this is the kind of card you want to hide away and protect, rather than use in tournament playing.

Back of the Ancient Egyptian Mew card (above) is also holographic. The movie program is a large-format magazine with a thick cover (left). A catalog page appears inside, featuring Pikablu items, as well as a few other new Pokémon we're not familiar with, yet.

PIKACHU (Lv17)
NOTES: Pika Birthday: On the Birthday of the user, a heads on a coin toss results in a +50 damage in addition to the initial 30 damage.

PIKACHU
NOTES: This is the card that will look familiar to anyone that's in a Pokémon league. It's the first card you earn, just for joining a league.

PIKACHU (Lv9)
NOTES: Second attack: Discard all energy cards attached to do 40 damage.

PIKACHU (Lv?)
NOTES: Second attack Pikachu pretends to be sleeping then attacks opponent for 30 damage.

DRAGONITE (Lv41)
NOTES: Pokémon Power: When activated it takes 2 damage counters off all user's Pokémon.

MEOWTH
NOTES: This card, with a darker gold border, could be found in specially marked boxes of Fruit Roll-Ups™. The other three cards are available in booster packs.

PIKACHU (LV13)
NOTES: We're not sure of the source for these cards, but most people refer to them as the "Ana" series.

MANKEY
NOTES: Pokémon Power: Can take a card from the top of either player's deck or prize cards and look at it.

KABUTO
NOTES: This special edition card features the Wizards "W" logo.

IMAKUNI?
NOTES: Decoy Imakuni, when played, confuses opponents activated Pokémon.

PIKABLU
DOUBLE WHITE STAR
NOTES: Water energy cards may be attached to add 10 damage. Limit 2.

KING SLOWPOKE (Lv37)
NOTES: Second attack: Player must recite "Should I really do it?" 3 times before initiating this 20 damage.

FLYING PIKACHU (Lv12)
NOTES: Second attack: 30 damage plus coin flip heads means next attack misses you, tails makes you paralyzed.

FLYING PIKACHU (Lv13)
NOTES: This Pikachu's electric shock is 10 points more damaging than level 12 Pikachu.

ARTICUNO
NOTES: Attack does 30 damage, but flip a coin heads to give each of the opposing bench Pokémon 10 damage.

ZAPDOS
NOTES: Coin flip as heads adds 30 damage to opposing bench's Pokémon tails gives plus 30 damage, also.

MOLTRES
NOTES: Damages 60 points, but you must flip a coin to see if you lose 1 of your fire energy cards of all attached to it.

DRAGONITE (Lv43)
NOTES: Pokémon Power: Take 1 card from the top of your deck, replace it with a card from your hand.

BULBASAUR DECK

The Bulbasaur Deck cards are all marked by a Bulbasaur icon to the bottom-right of the picture and marked with a special number in a circle in the bottom-right corner of the card. They're numbered 1-40, plus a special "004" Venusaur Holofoil. The cards pictured here are only a small sampling of the collection, but most of the cards are identical to those found in other sets.

BULBASAUR (Lv12)

BULBASAUR (Lv15)
NOTES: Second attack: Cure, during your turn you take one damage counter off of you.

IVYSAUR
NOTES: Attack gives opponent damage and allows one damage counter to be taken off of you.

VENUSAUR (#004)
NOTES: This is the only holofoil, making it the most collectible of the deck.

PIKACHU (Lv12)

PIKACHU (Lv16)
NOTES: Opponents attacks have 10 points subtracted from its damage after the first hit.

MEOWTH (Lv17)
NOTES: Second attack: Flip a coin x3, the amount of times it lands on heads equals to 10 points damage.

SQUIRTLE DECK

The Squirtle Deck cards are very similar to the Bulbasaur cards, but feature a Squirtle icon to the bottom-right of the picture. They're also marked with a special number in a circle in the bottom-right corner of the card, numbered 1-40, plus a special "009" Blastoise Holofoil. The cards pictured are only a small sampling of the collection, but most of the cards are identical to those found in other sets.

KOFFING

JYNX
NOTES: Double Slap, Flip coin x2, 10 damage per heads.

ELECTABUZZ

SQUIRTLE DECK
(continued)

RAICHU
NOTES: Second attack: Discard all energy cards attached to do 40 damage.

BILL'S 4 CARD DRAW
NOTES: Flip a coin, if heads draw 4 cards from your deck.

MAGNETON RETRIEVAL
NOTES: Flip coin, if heads, take any card on your bench with all cards attached to it and put it back in your hand.

SQUIRTLE (Lv14)

SQUIRTLE (Lv15)
NOTES: This attack gives x3 the damage on an opponent on your second turn..

WARTORTLE

ABRA

SPEAROW

GROWLITHE
NOTES: Second attack: Gives opponent 30 damage at the expense of 1 fire energy card.

JOLTEON

MAGMAR .

DOUBLE COLORLESS

EVOLUTION GUIDE

BASIC POKéMON	EVOLVED FORM 1	EVOLVED FORM 2
Bulbasaur (#1)	Ivysaur (#2)	Venusaur (#3)
Charmander (#4)	Charmeleon (#5)	Charizard (#6)
Squirtle (#7)	Wartortle (#8)	Blastoise (#9)
Caterpie (#10)	Metapod (#11)	Butterfree (#12)
Weedle (#13)	Kakuna (#14)	Beedrill (#15)
Pidgey (#16)	Pidgeotto (#17)	Pidgeot (#18)
Rattata (#19)	Raticate (#20)	
Spearow (#21)	Fearow (#22)	
Ekans (#23)	Arbok (#24)	
Pikachu (#25)	Raichu (#26)	
Sandshrew (#27)	Sandslash (#28)	
Nidoran(F) (#29)	Nidorina (#30)	Nidoqueen (#31)
Nidoran(M) (#32)	Nidorino (#33)	Nidoking (#34)
Clefairy (#35)	Clefable (#36)	
Vulpix (#37)	Ninetales (#38)	
Jigglypuff (#39)	Wigglytuff (#40)	
Zubat (#41)	Golbat (#42)	
Oddish (#43)	Gloom (#44)	Vileplume (#45)
Paras (#46)	Parasect (#47)	
Venonat (#48)	Venomoth (#49)	
Diglett (#50)	Dugtrio (#51)	
Meowth (#52)	Persian (#53)	
Psyduck (#54)	Golduck (#55)	
Mankey (#56)	Primeape (#57)	
Growlithe (#58)	Arcanine (#59)	
Poliwag (#60)	Poliwhirl (#61)	Poliwrath (#62)
Abra (#63)	Kadabra (#64)	Alakazam (#65)
Machop (#66)	Machoke (#67)	Machamp (#68)
Bellsprout (#69)	Weepinbell (#70)	Victreebel (#71)
Tentacool (#72)	Tentacruel (#73)	
Geodude (#74)	Graveller (#75)	Golem (#76)
Ponyta (#77)	Rapidash (#78)	
Magnemite (#81)	Magneton (#82)	
Doduo (#84)	Dodrio (#85)	
Seel (#86)	Dewgong (#87)	
Grimer (#88)	Muk (#89)	
Shellder (#90)	Cloyster (#91)	
Gastly (#92)	Haunter (#93)	Gengar (#94)

Drowzee (#96)   Hypno (#97)

Krabby (#98)   Kingler (#99)

Voltorb (#100)   Electrode (#101)

Exeggcute (#102)   Exeggutor (#103)

Cubone (#104)   Marowak (#105)

Koffing (#109)   Weezing (#110)

Rhyhorn (#111)   Rhydon (#112)

Horsea (#116)   Seadra (#117)

Goldeen (#118)   Seaking (#119)

Staryu (#120)   Starmie (#121)

Magikarp (#129)   Gyarados (#130)

Omanyte (#138)   Omastar (#139)

Kabuto (#140)   Kabutops (#141)

Dratini (#141)   Dragonair (#142)   Dragonite (#143)

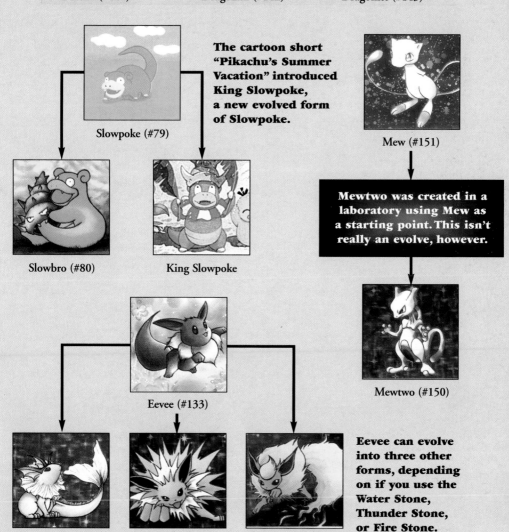

Slowpoke (#79)

The cartoon short "Pikachu's Summer Vacation" introduced King Slowpoke, a new evolved form of Slowpoke.

Mew (#151)

Mewtwo was created in a laboratory using Mew as a starting point. This isn't really an evolve, however.

Slowbro (#80)   King Slowpoke

Mewtwo (#150)

Eevee (#133)

Eevee can evolve into three other forms, depending on if you use the Water Stone, Thunder Stone, or Fire Stone.

Vaporeon (#134)   Jolteon (#135)   Flareon (#136)

EVOLUTION GUIDE

MASTER TCG POKéDEX

Gotta catch how many?!!

The chart on the following pages is handy for the daunting task of figuring out what cards are available for each of the 151+ Pokémon available. This chart was up-to-date at time of publication, but new cards are being released all the time.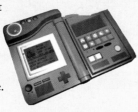

RARITY KEY:

C   Common (black circle)
U   Uncommon (black diamond)
R   Rare (black star)
H   Holograph (most are rare)
B   Border Holograph
SU   Super Uncommon (white diamond)
SR   Super Rare (white star)
G   Glossy Front (all vending and
           some promos)

SET KEY:

Basic (102 cards)
Jungle (48 cards JP; 64 cards US)
Fossil (48 cards JP; 62 cards US)
Team Rocket (65 cards)
Gym Leaders 1 (96 cards)
Gym Leaders 2 (98 cards)
Vending Machine 1 (36 cards)
Vending Machine 2 (36 cards)
Vending Machine 3 (36+16 cards)
Southern Islands (18 cards)
Promos (new ones available all the time)

JAPAN PRE-CONSTRUCTED DECKS:

Gym Deck 1=Brock's Deck
Gym Deck 2=Misty's Deck
Gym Deck 3=Lt. Surge's Deck
Gym Deck 4=Erica's Deck
Gym Deck 5=Sabrina's Deck
Gym Deck 6=Blaine's Deck

Note: This section is organized with Pokémon in alphabetical order.

SET	RARITY	LEVEL	HP
Abra (#63)			
Basic	C	10	30
Team Rocket	C	14	40
Vend 1	C	8	30
Gym Deck 5		12	40
Gym Deck 5		18	50
Gym 2	C	11	40
Aerodactyl (#142)			
Fossil	R	28	60
Vend 2	U	30	70
Alakazam (#65)			
Basic	R	42	80
Team Rocket	R	30	60
Vend 3	R	45	90
Gym Deck 5		44	80
Gym 2	H	44	80
Arbok (#24)			
Fossil	U	27	60
Team Rocket	R	25	60
Vend 3	U	30	60
Gym 2	R	44	90
Arcanine (#59)			
Basic	U	45	100
Gym Deck 6		42	90
Gym 2	H	42	90
Promo		34	70
Articuno (#144)			
Fossil	R	35	70
Vend 2	U	34	80
Beedrill (#15)			
Basic	R	32	80
Gym 2	H	34	80
Bellsprout (#69)			
Jungle	C	11	40
Gym Deck 4		12	40
Gym Deck 4		15	50
Gym 1	U	13	40
Gym 1	C	15	50
Vend 3	C	10	40
Blastoise (#9)			
Basic	R	52	100
Team Rocket	R	28	70
Promo	H	52	100
Bulbasaur (#1)			
Basic	C	13	40
Vend 1	U	15	50
Gym 1	U	15	50
Promo		15	50
Butterfree (#12)			
Jungle	U	28	70
South. Islands		37	80
Caterpie (#10)			
Basic	C	13	40
Vend 1		15	50

SET	RARITY	LEVEL	HP
Chansey (#113)			
Basic	R	55	120
Vend 1	U	40	100
Gym 2	SU	38	90
Charizard (#6)			
Basic	R	76	120
Team Rocket	R	38	80
Gym 2	H	50	100
Promo	H	76	120
Charmander (#4)			
Basic	C	10	50
Team Rocket	C	9	40
Vend 1	U	10	50
Gym Deck 6		18	50
Gym 2	C	16	50
Charmeleon (#5)			
Basic	U	32	80
Team Rocket	U	23	50
Gym 2	U	29	70
Clefable (#36)			
Jungle	R	34	70
Gym 1	R	35	70
Clefairy (#35)			
Basic	R	14	40
Vend 1	U	15	50
Gym Deck 4		17	50
Gym 1	U	16	50
Cloyster (#91)			
Fossil	U	25	50
Gym Deck 2		30	70
Cubone (#104)			
Jungle	C	13	40
Vend 3	C	14	40
Promo		15	50
Dewgong (#87)			
Basic	U	42	80
Vend 2	U	24	60
Gym 1	U	40	80
Diglett (#50)			
Basic	C	8	30
Team Tocket	C	15	40
Gym 1	C	13	40
Promo		16	50
Ditto (#132)			
Fossil	R	20	50
Vend 2	U	15	40
Gym 2		12	40
Dodrio (#85)			
Jungle	U	28	70
Vend 1	C	25	60
Gym Deck 6		26	70

	SET	RARITY	LEVEL	HP
Doduo (#84)				
	Basic	C	10	50
	Vend 1	C	10	40
	Gym Deck 6		17	50
	Gym 2	SR	15	50
	Gym 2	C	17	50
Dragonair (#148)				
	Basic	R	33	80
	Team Rocket	U	28	60
	Gym 1	R	32	80
Dragonite (#149)				
	Fossil	R	45	100
	Team Rocket	U	28	60
	Promo	H	41	100
Dratini (#147)				
	Basic	U	10	40
	Team Rocket	C	12	40
	Gym Deck 4		14	40
	Gym 1	U	14	40
	Promo		14	40
Drowzee (#96)				
	Basic	U	12	50
	Team Rocket	C	10	50
	Gym Deck 5		18	50
	Gym 2	C	15	50
Dugtrio (#51)				
	Basic	U	36	70
	Team Rocket	R	15	50
	Gym 2	R	27	60
	Promo		40	80
Eevee (#133)				
	Jungle	C	12	50
	Team Rocket	C	9	40
	Vend 1	C	5	30
	Gym 1	U	10	40
Ekans (#23)				
	Fossil	C	10	40
	Team Rocket	C	15	50
	Gym 2	C	17	50
Electabuzz (#125)				
	Basic	R	35	70
	Vend 2	C	22	60
	Gym Deck 3		22	60
	Gym 1	R	28	70
	Promo		20	60
	Promo		22	60
Electrode (#101)				
	Basic	R	40	80
	Jungle	R	42	90
	Team Rocket	U	24	40
	Gym Deck 3		33	70
Exeggcute (#102)				
	Jungle	C	15	50
	Gym Deck 4		12	40
	Gym 1	U	15	50

	SET	RARITY	LEVEL	HP
Exeggutor (#103)				
	Jungle	U	35	80
	Gym Deck 4		31	70
	Gym 1	U	31	70
	South. Islands		27	70
Farfetch'd (#83)				
	Basic	U	20	50
	Promo	U	20	50
Fearow (#22)				
	Jungle	U	27	70
	Vend 2	U	24	60
	Gym 1	R	30	70
Flareon (#136)				
	Jungle	R	28	70
	Team Rocket	U	23	50
Gastly (#92)				
	Basic	C	8	30
	Fossil	U	17	50
	Vend 3	C	13	40
	Gym Deck 5		9	30
	Gym Deck 5		16	50
	Gym 2	U	10	40
Gengar (#94)				
	Fossil	R	38	80
	Vend 3	R	40	80
	Gym Deck 5		42	90
	Gym 2	H	39	80
Geodude (#74)				
	Fossil	C	16	50
	Vend 1	C	15	50
	Gym Deck 1		13	40
	Gym Deck 1		17	50
	Gym 1	C	13	40
	Gym 1	C	15	50
Gloom (#44)				
	Jungle	U	22	60
	Team Rocket	U	21	50
	Gym Deck 4		28	70
	Gym 1	U	24	60
Golbat (#42)				
	Fossil	U	29	60
	Team Rocket	R	25	50
	Vend 1	C	25	50
	Gym 1	U	30	70
	Gym 2	U	27	60
Goldeen (#118)				
	Jungle	C	12	40
	Gym Deck 2		8	30
	Gym Deck 2		10	40
	Gym 1	C	10	40
Golduck (#55)				
	Fossil	U	27	70
	Team Rocket	U	23	60
	Gym 1	R	32	70
	Vend 3	U	28	70
	Gym 2	R	33	70

SET	RARITY	LEVEL	HP
Golem (#76)			
Fossil	U	36	80
Gym Deck 1		40	90
Gym 1	R	40	90
Vend 3	R	37	80
Graveller (#75)			
Fossil	U	29	60
Gym Deck 1		40	90
Vend 2	U	28	60
Gym 1	U	32	70
Vend 3	C	27	60
Grimer (#88)			
Fossil	C	17	50
Team Rocket	C	10	40
Vend 2	C	15	50
Gym 2	C	19	50
Growlithe (#58)			
Basic	U	16	60
Vend 3	C	16	50
Gym Deck 6		17	50
Gym Deck 6		20	60
Gym 2	C	15	50
Gyarados (#130)			
Basic	R	41	100
Team Rocket	R	31	70
Gym1	R	42	100
Gym2	H	40	90
Haunter (#93)			
Basic	U	22	60
Fossil	R	17	50
Vend 3	U	30	60
Vend 3	U	26	70
Gym Deck 5		31	71
Gym 2	U	20	50
Hitmonchan (#107)			
Basic	R	33	70
Vend 2	U	23	50
Gym 1	R	29	60
Hitmonlee (#106)			
Fossil	R	30	60
Vend 2	U	23	50
Horsea (#116)			
Fossil	C	19	60
Gym Deck 2		10	40
Gym 1	C	10	40
Gym 1	C	16	50
Vend 3	C	20	40
Hypno (#97)			
Fossil	R	36	90
Team Rocket	R	26	60
Vend 3	U	30	60
Gym Deck 5		31	70
Gym 2	U	31	70
Ivysaur (#2)			
Basic	U	20	60
Gym 2	U	22	60
South. Islands		23	60

SET	RARITY	LEVEL	HP
Jigglypuff (#39)			
Jungle	C	14	60
Gym 1	C	13	50
South. Islands		10	40
Promo		12	50
Jolteon (#135)			
Jungle	R	29	70
Team Tocket	U	23	50
Gym 1	R	32	70
Promo		32	70
Jynx (#124)			
Basic	U	23	70
Vend 2	U	18	50
Gym Deck 5		20	60
Gym 2	U	21	60
Promo		32	70
Kabuto (#140)			
Fossil	C	9	30
Vend 2	U	22	50
Kabutops (#141)			
Fossil	R	30	60
Kadabra (#64)			
Basic	U	38	60
Team Rocket	U	24	50
Vend 3	U	39	60
Vend 3	C	40	70
Gym Deck 5		41	70
Gym 2	U	41	70
Kakuna (#14)			
Basic	U	23	80
Vend1	U	20	60
Gym 2	U	21	60
Kangaskhan (#115)			
Jungle	R	40	90
Vend 3	C	36	80
Gym 2	U	36	80
Promo		12	40
Promo		38	80
King Slowpoke			
South Islands	B	36	70
Kingler (#99)			
Fossil	U	27	60
Vend 3	U	33	80
Koffing (#109)			
Basic	C	13	50
Team Rocket	C	12	40
Vend 3	C	16	50
Gym 2	C	10	40
Gym 2	U	15	50
Krabby (#98)			
Fossil	C	20	50
Vend 2	C	17	40
Lady-Ba			
South Islands	B	12	40

SET	RARITY	LEVEL	HP
Lapras (#131)			
Fossil	R	31	80
Vend 2	C	24	60
South Islands		25	70
Lickitung (#108)			
Jungle	U	26	90
Vend 1	U	20	60
Gym 1	U	24	80
South Islands		25	70
Machamp (#68)			
Basic	R	67	100
Team Rocket	U	30	70
Vend 3	R	54	90
Gym 2	H	50	100
Machoke (#67)			
Basic	U	40	80
Team Rocket	U	28	60
Vend 2	C	28	70
Vend 3	C	24	60
Gym 2	U	36	80
Machop (#66)			
Basic	C	20	50
Team Rocket	C	24	50
Vend 2	C	18	50
Gym 2	C	18	50
Magikarp (#129)			
Basic	U	8	30
Team Rocket	C	6	30
Gym 1	C	5	30
Gym 2	C	9	30
Magmar (#126)			
Basic	U	24	50
Fossil	U	31	70
Vend 3	U	27	60
Gym Deck 6		29	60
Gym 2	U	29	60
Magnemite (#81)			
Basic	C	13	40
Team Rocket	C	12	40
Vend 2	C	15	40
Gym Deck 3		10	30
Gym Deck 3		12	40
Gym 1	U	10	30
Gym 1	C	12	40
Magneton (#82)			
Basic	R	28	60
Fossil	R	35	80
Team Rocket	R	26	60
Vend 2	U	30	70
Gym Deck 3		30	70
Gym 1	R	30	70
Mankey (#56)			
Jungle	C	7	30
Team Rocket	C	14	40
Gym Deck 1		10	40
Gym 1	C	12	40
Gym 2	C	14	40

SET	RARITY	LEVEL	HP
Marowak (#105)			
Jungle	U	26	60
Vend 2	U	25	60
Meowth (#52)			
Jungle	C	15	50
Team Rocket	C	10	40
Gym 2	U	12	40
Gym 2	C	17	50
Promo		13	50
Promo		14	50
Metapod (#11)			
Basic	C	21	70
Vend 1	U	20	70
Mew/Myuu (#151)			
Fossil	R	23	50
South Island	B	5	30
Promo		8	40
Promo		8	40
Promo		25	50
Mewtwo (#150)			
Basic	R	53	60
Vend 1	R	30	60
Vend 1	U	54	80
Vend 3	C	67	80
Gym 2	H	35	70
Promo		54	80
Promo		60	70
Promo		60	70
Moltres (#146)			
Fossil	R	35	70
Vend 2	U	37	80
Gym 1	R	26	60
Gym 2	H	44	90
Mr.Mime (#122)			
Jungle	R	28	40
Vend 1	U	20	50
Gym Deck 5		90	60
Gym 2	C	20	50
Muk (#89)			
Fossil	R	34	70
Team Rocket	U	25	60
Gym 2	R	38	80
Nidoking (#34)			
Basic	R	48	90
Gym 2	H	58	120
Promo		50	100
Nidoqueen (#31)			
Jungle	R	43	90
Gym 2	R	51	100
Nidoran(F) (#29)			
Jungle	C	13	60
Vend 1	C	12	50
Gym 2	C	11	50

SET	RARITY	LEVEL	HP
Nidoran(M) (#32)			
Basic	C	20	40
Vend 1	C	22	50
Gym 2	C	14	40
Nidorina (#30)			
Jungle	U	24	70
Vend 3	U	22	60
Gym 2	U	35	80
Nidorino (#33)			
Basic	U	25	60
Vend 3	U	23	60
Gym 2	U	32	70
Ninetales (#38)			
Basic	R	32	80
Gym 1	R	30	70
Gym Deck 6		27	60
Gym 2	R	27	60
Oddish (#43)			
Jungle	C	8	50
Team Rocket	C	21	50
Gym Deck 4		12	40
Gym Deck 4		15	50
Gym 1	C	10	40
Gym 1	C	15	50
Omanyte (#138)			
Fossil	C	19	40
Vend 2	U	20	50
Vend 3	U	22	50
Omastar (#139)			
Fossil	U	32	70
Vend 3	R	36	80
Onix (#95)			
Basic	C	12	90
Gym Deck 1		30	70
Gym Deck 1		41	100
Vend 2	U	25	70
Gym 1	C	41	100
South Islands		40	90
Promo		41	100
Paras (#46)			
Jungle	C	8	40
Vend 1	C	15	50
Gym 1	C	17	50
Parasect (#47)			
Jungle	U	28	60
Vend 1	C	29	60
Persian (#53)			
Jungle	U	25	70
Team Rocket	C	28	60
Gym 2	H	23	60
Promo		28	60
Pidgeot (#18)			
Jungle	R	40	80
South Islands		39	70

SET	RARITY	LEVEL	HP
Pidgeotto (#17)			
Basic	R	36	60
Vend 3	U	38	60
Gym 2	R	34	60
Pidgey (#16)			
Basic	C	8	40
Vend 1	C	10	50
Gym 2	U	9	40
Gym 2	C	15	50
Pikablu			
South Islands	B	30	60
Promo	G	17	50
Pikachu (#25)			
Basic	C	12	40
Jungle	C	14	50
Vend 1	U	5	30
Vend 1	R	13	50
Gym Deck 3		10	40
Gym Deck 3		15	50
Gym 1	C	10	40
Promo	G	9	40
Promo		12	40
Promo		13	50
Promo		16	60
Promo		16	60
Promo		17	50
Pinsir (#127)			
Jungle	R	24	60
Vend 1	U	15	50
Gym 2	R	27	70
Poliwag (#60)			
Basic	C	13	40
Vend 1	C	15	50
Gym Deck 2		15	50
Gym 1	C	16	50
Poliwhirl (#61)			
Basic	U	28	60
Vend 1	U	30	70
Gym 1	U	37	70
Poliwrath (#61)			
Basic	R	48	90
Vend 1	U	40	80
Gym 2	R	43	90
Ponyta (#77)			
Basic	C	10	40
Team Rocket	C	15	50
Vend 3	C	8	40
Gym Deck 6		11	40
Gym Deck 6		13	50
Gym 2	C	13	50
Porygon (#137)			
Basic	U	12	30
Team Rocket	C	20	40
Vend 1	C	18	40
Gym Deck 5		17	40
Gym 2	C	17	40
Promo	H	15	50

MASTER TCG POKéDEX

SET	RARITY	LEVEL	HP
Primeape (#57)			
Jungle	U	35	70
Team Rocket	U	23	60
Gym 1	U	32	70
South Islands		26	60
Psyduck (#54)			
Fossil	C	15	50
Team Rocket	C	16	50
Gym Deck 2		15	50
Gym 1	C	16	60
Gym 2	C	16	50
Raichu (#26)			
Basic	R	40	80
Fossil	R	45	90
Vend 2	U	32	70
Gym Deck 3		32	70
Gym 2	H	38	80
Rapidash (#78)			
Jungle	U	33	70
Team Rocket	C	24	60
Vend 1	U	30	60
Gym Deck 6		31	70
Gym 2	U	31	70
Raticate (#20)			
Basic	U	41	60
Team Rocket	C	25	50
Gym Deck 3		32	70
Gym 1	U	33	60
South Islands		25	60
Rattata (#19)			
Basic	C	9	30
Team Rocket	C	12	40
Vend 1	C	15	50
Gym Deck 3		10	40
Gym 1	C	7	30
Rhydon (#112)			
Jungle	U	48	100
Gym Deck 1		38	80
Gym 1	R	38	80
Vend 3	U	37	80
Rhyhorn (#111)			
Jungle	C	18	70
Gym Deck 1		25	60
Gym 1	C	27	70
Gym 2	C	26	60
Sandshrew (#27)			
Basic	C	12	40
Gym Deck 1		13	40
Vend 2	C	15	40
Gym 1	C	20	50
Sandslash (#28)			
Fossil	U	33	70
Gym Deck 1		26	60
Gym 1	U	34	70
Vend 3	C	35	70

SET	RARITY	LEVEL	HP
Scyther (#123)			
Jungle	R	25	70
Gym 1	R	23	60
Vend 3	U	23	60
Seadra (#117)			
Fossil	U	23	60
Gym 1	R	30	70
Vend 3	U	26	70
Seaking (#119)			
Jungle	U	28	70
Gym Deck 2		24	70
Seel (#86)			
Basic	U	12	60
Gym Deck 2		20	60
Vend 2	C	10	50
Gym 1	C	14	50
Shellder (#90)			
Fossil	C	8	30
Gym Deck 2		10	40
Vend 2	C	16	50
Slowbro (#80)			
Fossil	U	26	60
Team Rocket	R	27	60
Vend 3	C	35	90
Gym 2	U	29	70
Slowpoke (#79)			
Fossil	C	18	50
Team Rocket	C	16	50
Gym 2	C	15	50
Promo		9	40
Snorlax (#143)			
Jungle	R	20	90
Vend 1	U	35	90
Gym 2	R	40	90
Promo	H	50	100
Spearow (#21)			
Jungle	C	13	50
Vend 2	U	12	40
Gym Deck 3		8	30
Gym 1	C	17	50
Squirtle (#7)			
Basic	C	8	40
Team Rocket	C	16	50
Vend 1	U	15	50
Starmie (#121)			
Basic	C	28	60
Gym Deck 2		35	80
Staryu (#120)			
Basic	C	15	40
Gym Deck 2		16	40
Gym Deck 2		20	50
Gym 1	C	16	40
Vend 3	C	17	50
Promo		16	40

SET	RARITY	LEVEL	HP
Tangela (#114)			
Basic	C	8	50
Vend 2	C	15	50
Gym Deck 4		21	60
Gym 1	C	21	60
Gym 2	C	16	50
Tauros (#128)			
Jungle	U	32	60
Vend 3	C	35	70
Gym 2	C	34	70
Tentacool (#72)			
Fossil	C	10	30
Gym Deck 2		12	40
Gym 1	U	16	50
Promo		16	50
Tentacruel (#73)			
Fossil	U	21	60
Gym Deck 2		30	70
Gym 1	R	30	70
South Islands		30	60
Togepi			
South Island	B	10	40
Promo	G	8	30
Vaporeon (#134)			
Jungle	R	42	80
Team Rocket	U	28	60
Venomoth (#49)			
Jungle	U	28	70
Vend 2	C	22	60
Gym 2	C	13	40
Venonat (#48)			
Jungle	C	12	40
Vend 3	C	15	50
Gym 2	C	13	40
Venus (#3)			
Basic	R	67	100
Gym 2	H	45	90
Promo	H	64	100
Promo	H	67	100
Victrebel (#71)			
Jungle	R	42	80
Gym Deck 4		37	80
Gym 1	R	37	80
Vileplume (#45)			
Jungle	R	35	80
Team Rocket	R	29	60
Gym Deck 4		34	80
Gym 1	R	34	80
South Islands	B	30	70
Voltorb (#100)			
Basic	C	10	40
Team Rocket	C	13	40
Vend 2	C	8	30
Gym Deck 3		12	40
Gym Deck 3		15	50
Gym 1	C	12	40

SET	RARITY	LEVEL	HP
Vulpix (#37)			
Basic	C	11	50
Gym Deck1		10	40
Gym 1	C	10	40
Gym 1	U	16	50
Vend 3	C	13	50
Gym Deck 6		9	40
Gym Deck 6		18	50
Gym 2	C	9	40
Wartortle (#8)			
Basic	U	22	70
Team Rocket	U	21	60
South Islands		26	60
Weedle (#13)			
Basic	C	12	40
Vend 1	C	15	50
Gym 2	C	13	40
Weepinbell (#70)			
Jungle	U	28	70
Gym Deck 4		30	70
Gym 1	U	26	60
Vend 3	U	23	60
Weezing (#110)			
Fossil	U	27	60
Team Rocket	R	24	60
Vend 3	U	26	60
Gym 2	U	31	70
Wigglytuff (#40)			
Jungle	R	36	80
Vend 1	U	40	90
Zapdos (#145)			
Basic	R	64	90
Fossil	R	40	80
Vend 2	U	28	70
Gym 2	H	34	70
Zubat (#41)			
Fossil	C	10	40
Team Rocket	C	9	40
Vend 1	C	12	40
Gym Deck 1		5	30
Gym 1	C	11	40
Gym 2	C	14	40

MASTER TCG POKéDEX

The world of the Pokémon Trading Card Game can be confusing and frustrating for budding Pokémon Masters. There are so many rules to learn! And many of the rules involve strange new terms that are custom only to this game. How can anyone keep up with all of it?

Don't worry! We've got you covered! Just keep a copy of this strategy guide handy when you run across some Trainers speaking "Poke-Lingo" and you will fit right in! Whether they are trying to explain the current state of the localized Turbo Wiggly Metagame to you, or simply asking your opinion on Trainer Ratios in a Fossilized Potpourri deck, you should be able to roll with the conversation and drop a few Lingo phrases of your own. You know you've got them thinking when they have to check their own strategy guides to translate your own brilliant insights!

"Active Pokémon" • A player's active Pokémon is their attacking and defending Pokémon card. Each player must choose only one of their in-play monsters as their active Pokémon–All other in-play monsters are considered to be on the bench.

"Archetype" • Archetype defines a general class of decks. Each deck within the archetype will maintain a common set of themes and core cards that set it apart from other, different archetypes. Haymaker, Rain Dance, and Damage Swap are all examples of deck archetypes.

"Asleep" • Asleep Pokémon are not allowed to attack or retreat. Asleep Pokémon have the chance to pass a coin flip at the end of each player's turn in order to wake up. See "Pokémon Ailment".

"Attach" • Most cards in the game are put into play on the table. Many of these cards require a target card to be in-play first before they can used (like an evolution card). These cards will be be "attached" to their target card after played. Simply place the card on top, or underneath the target card and consider the two connected.

"Attack Energy Requirement" • Attack Energy Requirement is the amount (and type) of Energy required to be attached to an Active Pokémon in order for it to use an Attack Move. Attack Moves will show this as a series of color symbols printed to the left of the Attack Name.

"Attack Damage" • Attack damage is the number of points of damage an Attack Move inflicts upon the Defending Pokémon. Attack damage will be printed to the right of the Attack Name, and may involve some calculations based on the Attack Text.

"Attack Move" • The text written on a Pokémon's card that shows what it does when it attacks. (The Attack Move is broken down into Attack Energy Requirement, Attack Name, Attack Damage, and Attack Text.)

"Attack Name" • Simple word or phrase the names the Attack Move and is printed on the card between the move's Attack Energy Requirement and Attack Damage.

"Attack Text" • Attack Text represents additional requirements, benefits, penalties, and/or descriptions that some Attack Moves have. Attack Text will be printed on the Pokémon Card under the Attack Name.

"Basic Energy card" • Basic Energy cards are a subclass of a broader set of cards referred to as Energy cards. Although there are several additional cards that define themselves as "Energy cards", only 6 very special cards are considered "Basic" Energy cards. They are the Fighting, Fire, Grass, Lightning, Psychic, and Water energy cards.

"Basic Pokémon card" • Basic Pokémon cards are a subclass of a broader set of cards referred to as Pokémon cards. Although every card that describes a monster in the game is a Pokémon card (including all Evolution cards), only those cards that state "Basic Pokémon" in the upper left corner are considered "Basic" Pokémon cards.

"Bench" • A player's Bench is one of the distinct locations on their side of the game table that should contain TCG cards. The Bench is used for deploying additional Pokémon cards into play so that fainted Active Pokémon can be easily replaced. There are slots available for 5 Pokémon on a player's bench.

"Broken" • This is a common TCG term that describes a card or deck that is extremely strong and nearly impossible to defend against. They are said to "break" the game and make it less fun for everyone to compete. "Rain Dance is a broken deck."

"Card Advantage" • Cards that allow a player to have as many options at any one particular time are said to give that player "card advantage". Professor Oak and Bill are great examples of trainer cards that provide card advantage.

"Color" • When used in reference to Pokémon and Energy cards, the "color" will be one of 7 types: Fighting, Fire, Grass, Lightning, Psychic, Water or Colorless.

"Confused" • Confused Pokémon are allowed to attack and retreat with the passing of a coin flip, but face consequences in the coin flip fails. See Pokémon Ailment.

"Cost" • Primarily when discussing Clefairy/Clefable's Metronome attack move, "cost" represents all requirements that MUST be fulfilled prior to using a particular attack move. Attack Energy Requirements are considered "costs". Also, any Attack Text that uses the "in order to" template is considered a "cost". ("Discard 1 Fire Energy card in order to use this attack.")

"Damage Counter" • When a TCG card discusses a "Damage Counter" it is always describing a unit of 10 damage. Regardless of how much damage a player decides that each color of glass bead shall represent, "Damage Counters" are 10 damage each.

"Damage Swap" • Damage Swap is a deck archetype based on Alakazam's Pokémon Power. The essence of this deck is to Damage Swap all damage off of a strong attacker onto bigger monsters on your bench so that the attacker can stay in battle longer.

"Deck" • Deck is the pile of cards you draw from during the course of the game. It is synonymous with "Draw Pile".

"Deck Manipulation" • Cards that allow a player to man-handle their draw piles to assist them getting the optimum card at the optimum time provide "deck manipulation". Computer Search and Pokémon Trader are good examples.

"Deck your opponent" • If your goal is to "Deck your opponent" you are hoping that they run out of cards to draw from their Deck (causing them to lose the game at the beginning of their turn when they are required to draw a card, but can't).

"Defending Pokémon" • All Pokémon cards that refer to "Defending Pokémon" are describing the opponent's Active Pokémon only. Benched Pokémon are never "Defending Pokémon" regardless of whether they receive attack damage or not.

"Discard pile" • The Discard pile is the area of the table where a player will place expended Trainer cards or K-O'd Pokémon and Energy cards.

"Draw Pile" • Draw Pile is the pile of cards you draw from during the course of the game. It is synonymous with "Deck".

"Energy" • Energy is a unit of power. It will be one of 7 different "colors" or types: Fighting, Fire, Grass, Lightning, Psychic, Water or Colorless.

"Energy card" • An Energy card provides "Energy". Any card that describes itself as an Energy card (including a few unique Trainer or Pokémon cards) can be the target of abilities that specifically affect "Energy cards". Do not confuse "Energy Card" with "Basic Energy Card".

"Evolution card" • A card you can play on top of a Basic Pokémon card (or sometimes on top of another Evolution card) to make it stronger.

"Graveyard" • Graveyard is synonymous with "Discard Pile". It originates from the Magic Trading Card Game.

"Hand" • Each player will maintain several cards available for use in their "Hand".These cards are typically drawn from the player's deck, but may also be placed there from play in certain situation.

"Haymaker" • Haymaker is a deck archetype based on fast, efficient basic Pokémon like Hitmonchan and Electabuzz.The essence of this deck is to beat the opponent up as swiftly and methodically as possible.

"Hit Points" • Hit Points indicate a monster's overall toughness. Damage on a Pokémon must be equal to or greater than its Hit Points in order for that Pokémon to be Knocked-Out.

"Hosed" • Hosed generally refers to a situation in which a card or player can not perform adequately. A Rain Dance deck with no Water energy cards included is "hosed".

"In-Play" • All Pokémon face up on the game table are considered "in-play". Both Active and Bench areas of the table are considered "in-play".

"Knocked Out" • When a Pokémon is sent to the discard pile from attack damage it is "Knocked Out" (or "K-O'd" for short). One of the main objects of the game is to knock-out as many of your opponents Pokémon as possible.

"Metagame" • The Metagame describes a local tournament or casual game play location's best decks. Every location will seem to have particular players using particular decks that are dominant. This is the Metagame. And this is what other players will try to specifically defend against.

"Mulligan" • On your initial 7 card draw, if you have no Basic Pokémon cards, you have a "Mulligan" and need to reshuffle and draw again.

"Paralyzed" • Paralyzed Pokémon are not allowed to attack or retreat. However, Paralysis automatically ends after one full turn. See Pokémon Ailment.

"Pokémon" • The English word for a Pocket Monster. Pokémon is the generic name given to the class of unique creatures that do all the battling in the card game.

"Pokémon Ailments" • Asleep, Confused, Paralyzed and Poisoned are all Pokémon Ailments. They have unique rules describing their effects, and are typically detrimental to the Pokémon that is inflicted with the Ailment.

"Pokémon Power" • Different than an attack move, a Pokémon Power is a special class of abilities that some Pokémon possess.There are always very specific rules for using them and most of those rules are printed on the card with the Pokémon Power.

"Poisoned" • Poisoned Pokémon are allowed to attack and retreat, but at the end of each player's turn a Poisoned Pokémon will take 10 additional damage from the Poison condition. See Pokémon Ailment.

"Potpourri" • Potpourri is a deck archetype designed by Scott Gerhardt that optimizes Weakness/Resistance match-ups by including a very wide variety of strong basic Pokémon and a boat-load of deck manipulation to get them into play.

"Prize Cards" • At the beginning of a Pokémon TCG match, each player will set aside 6 "prize cards" from their own deck. Collecting all of these cards represent one of the three main objectives in the Pokémon TCG.

"Rain Dance" • Rain Dance is a deck archetype based on Blastoise's Pokémon Power. The essence of this deck is to get Blastoise into play as early as possible and then Rain Dance multiple Water energy cards onto your attackers immediately for big attacks.

"Ratios" • Many of the cards in the Pokémon TCG require other, different cards in order

POKéLINGO

to be used properly. Since a deck must be exactly 60 cards in size, much of the player's concern will be optimizing "ratios" of these combo cards so that they have the best chance of being drawn, and in the correct order. A 4:3:2 Ratio for Pokémon evolution cards is pretty standard (4 Basic Pokémon: 3 Stage 1 cards : 2 Stage 2 cards)

"Resistance" • Resistance is a specific attribute that must be considered when calculating overall attack damage. A Pokémon that has a resistance to an opposing Pokémon's Type will take 30 less damage from all attacks by that resisted Pokémon.

"Retreat Cost" • Retreat Costs are printed on Pokémon cards on the bottom. Once satisfied (by discarding energy cards until the Retreat Cost has been satisfied) an Active Pokémon can move back to the safety of its bench so that a different in-play Pokémon can take the point.

"Sudden Death" • In rare, extreme situations it may be necessary for a game to conclude with a "Sudden Death" match. This is played identically to a normal full game, except that only 1 prize card for each player is used.

"Trainer card" • Trainer cards are a class of cards that provide for interesting results based on the rules printed on them. Pokémon matches would get pretty boring without the use of these cards in a player's deck.

"Trash" • Trash is synonymous with "Discard Pile". It originates from the Pocket Monsters Card Game.

"Turbo" • Any deck that makes heavy use of Card Advantage and Deck Manipulation to get a combo into play as quick as possible is referred to as "Turbo". Typical examples include Turbo Rain Dance decks, Turbo Venucenter decks, and Turbo Wiggly decks.

"Type" • Energy and Pokémon come in 6 Basic "Types" but may also be non-typed (Colorless). See "Basic Energy card" for the names of these 6 Basic Types. This is synonymous with "Color".

"Venucenter" • Venucenter is a deck archetype based on Venusaur's Pokémon Power Energy Trans used in combination with the Pokémon Center Trainer card. By first transferring all Grass energy cards onto an undamaged Pokémon in play the Pokémon Center can be used without fear of discarding those energy cards. (Only energy cards from damaged Pokémon are discarded when using Pokémon Center.)

"Weakness" • Weakness is a specific attribute that must be considered when calculating overall attack damage. A Pokémon that has a weakness to an opposing Pokémon's Type will take double damage from all attacks by that dominant Pokémon.

"Wiggly" • Wiggly decks are focused on Wigglytuff and its "Do the Wave" attack move. With a full bench, "Do the Wave" is one of the most cost effective attack moves in the game, and Wiggly decks make use of this fact by including plenty of other disruptive elements in place of unneeded energy cards.

FURBY OFFICIAL TRAINER'S GUIDE

by J. Douglas Arnold and his team of experts
144 Pages • $12.95 • ISBN 1-884364-26-8

This clear, concise, easy-to-read guide will take readers into the mind of their Furby, to help them better understand their personalities, needs, and the Furbish™ language. Nearly 100 pictures and step-by-step instructions will have Furby owners mastering their pets in no time. Includes English-to-Furbish™ and Furbish™-to-English dictionaries, an all new Collector's Guide, an updated Scrapbook with exclusive rare photos, a guide to Furby Babies, and much more!

ORDER FORM

VIDEO GAME HINT AND SECRETS BOOKS

SEND TO:

Name _____

Address _____

City _____ State ____ Zip _____

Phone ( ) _____

Method of Payment:

( ) Check/Money Order   ( ) MasterCard/Visa/Amex

Credit card users complete card information:

Card # _____ Expires: _____

Cardholder's Signature: _____

TITLE	ISBN	PRICE	x QTY	= TOTAL
Furby Official Trainer's Guide	(1-884364-26-8)	$12.95	_____	$ _____
Clock Tower: The Struggle Within Official Guide	(1-884364-28-4)	$12.95	_____	$ _____
Pokémon Trainer's Guide	(1-884364-25-X)	$12.95	_____	$ _____
Pokémon Trading Card Game Player's Guide	(1-884364-50-0)	$12.95	_____	$ _____
Pokémon TCG Fossil Exp. Player's Guide	(1-884364-39-X)	$12.95	_____	$ _____
Metal Gear Solid Survival Guide	(1-884364-31-4)	$12.95	_____	$ _____
Armored Core: Project Phantasma Official Guide	(1-884364-32-2)	$12.95	_____	$ _____
Best of Maui (hardbound Maui island visitor guide)		$12.00	_____	$ _____

Sub-Total: $ _____

Air Shipping ($4.00 U.S. and Canada TOTAL; $5.00 Foreign PER BOOK in U.S. FUNDS): $ _____

Total: $ _____

MAIL, FAX OR SEND TO:
SANDWICH ISLANDS PUBLISHING
P.O. Box 10669, Lahaina, HI 96761
Fax: (808) 661-2715
Phone Orders: (808) 661-8195

See our web site for updated information, detailed listings, and special offers!

www.gamebooks.com

Pokémon TCG Fossil Expansion Player's Guide